E.J.KELLY

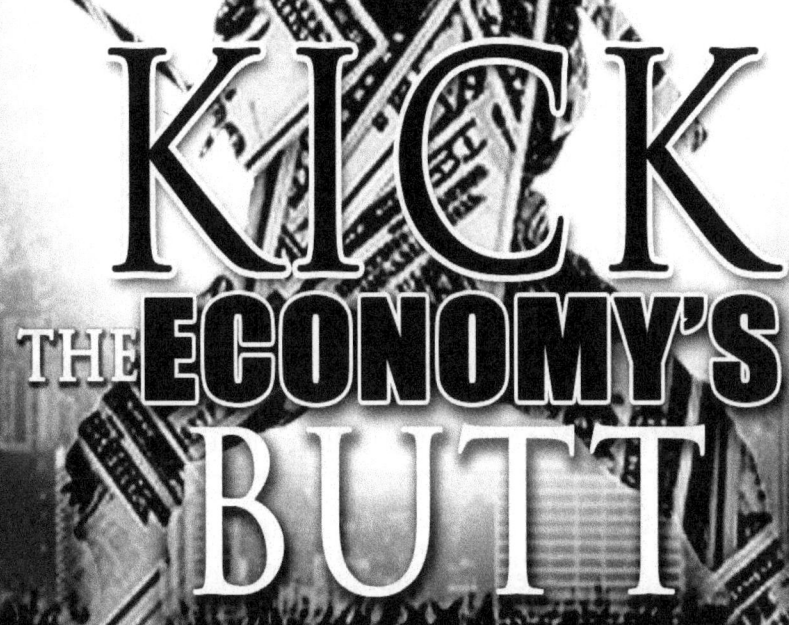

KICK
THE ECONOMY'S
BUTT

A Ninja Guide for Small Business

Prologue

On any given day, you can find me on a different terrace sipping a café Americano. It is my routine, and the moderated java is the drug of choice. I never got used to the strong coffee or espresso available in Europe.

One particular morning I was reading about the magnificent cathedral called the Sagrada Família in Barcelona. The building's construction started in 1882, and to this day it is still incomplete. Designed by Gaudí and designated as a World Heritage Site, it is a sight to behold, but the ongoing construction nightmare. The projected completion date is 2026, the anniversary of Gaudí's death.

I have doubts.

As I finish the article, my mobile rings. My friend is inquiring what I am doing. I said I was doing the usual…I was drinking coffee, people watching and rag reading. Out of the blue he asks, "Can you get to Barcelona this weekend"? Incredulously, I enquired whether he was reading the same article. He said no, he needed a break and wanted to hook up with me.
Four days later, on a gorgeous sunny day, I am sipping an Americano in front of the incredible yet incomplete masterpiece of Gaudí.

It's apparent that the thing will never be finished in my

lifetime. Reflecting over my coffee, I was amazed about how I happened to be in this place. How did all this happen? How did I get here? How on a whim, I was able to join a friend in an exotic city to continue my practice of sipping café in another outdoor café?

The journey was both chaotic and smooth, but always fun.

If you are seeking an independent and hassle-free life, this guide is for you!

Contents

Part One

Definition: Of The Word Ninja In The Title

There is a lot of contemporary use of this term lately. Historically, Ninjas were a group of well-trained mercenaries and spies whose origins began in the feudal times in Japan. They essentially were responsible for covert operations including but not limited to infiltration, sabotage, espionage and sometime assassinations.

In this book, there will be no killing or destruction. Instead, you will be privy to the stealth ideas and methods used by the author to start and control 11 different small businesses. No need to jump fences, kick in doors or go crazy. Just sit back, relax and learn and discover a few tricks from this valuable resource about getting into your own business.

Definition: Iceman

Definition: "Iceman" is an independent creative entrepreneur. It is used throughout this book. Icemen make things happen. The term applies to both genders. An 'iceman' is a 'hustler' or a serial entrepreneur.

"Action is the foundational key to all success."
Pablo Picasso

Dedication

Having children makes you more human. You realize the world isn't just about you anymore. You now think of yours and others—you treat people better. This is truly being more human.

Thanks AMK and CVK — this is dedicated to you.

1. Why This Book?

"Formal Education will make you a living; self-education will make you a fortune."
- Jim Rohn, American writer

I wrote this book because, over the years, I created some genuinely cool businesses. I survived in some of the most insane economic environments we have ever seen, from the savings bank scandals and the tech bubble right through the latest fiasco starting in 2008. I helped friends take control of their destiny. Sharing my hard-earned experience might make the path easier for other people.

I am no business guru; I never worked for a big corporation. I worked as an employee in only five short-term jobs, yet I am a successful entrepreneur.

Most graduating college students want a job that leads to promotions. They are often disappointed. Graduates all over America, including my own daughter, find it extremely difficult to find a job in line with their education and career goals.

It has been two years since my daughter graduated with honors, yet she is still working in a variety of dead-end jobs.

She and many of her fellow graduates take jobs for survival while waiting for the ultimate career position. This results in an outrageous number of highly educated citizens working 'temporarily' as restaurant servers, retail salespeople, or taxi drivers while trying to pay off major debt acquired on the way to a diploma. Yet those survival jobs could be the key to a successful future for my daughter, for her classmates, and for you.

When I was younger, I also took jobs just to survive. These full-time, non-career jobs turned out to be important for my success. They gave me valuable experience and allowed me to think about my working life. I chose was to put the experiences learned from these early jobs into starting my own businesses. By taking control of my own destiny, I significantly increased my chances for survival. You can do the same.

I first thought about writing a book about U.S. startups as a learning guide for the foreign students taking Business English. However, I realized a broader audience could benefit from my guide. Many people would like to start a business but don't know how to do it.

I had friends who were stuck in jobs that offered no chance of being promoted. They watched and wondered how I was succeeding. One or two friends quit their jobs to come work for me. In one heartbreaking situation, a friend working for a large corporation was suddenly fired. He had no idea what to do. He sought my advice, and I am happy to report he now runs a medical billing service and is in charge of his own life. Through this book, I would like to help others the way I helped him.

2. Introduction: Thoughts from an 'Iceman'

"Try not to become a man of success, but rather try to become a man of value."
- Albert Einstein

The startups in this book are real. When I describe the challenges and satisfactions of starting your own gig, I speak from experience.

To realize your dream, you don't have to be a whiz with numbers or a Harvard graduate. You need only a little guidance and a sprinkle of inspiration. I started and maintained all of the businesses described in this book until I pulled the exit trigger.

I believe the best reason to start a business is to gain freedom and control. Coming out of my teens, I realized that running my own business was the future because there was no way to gain control of my leisure time.

Starting and running a business is a creative endeavor that allows you to generate value for yourself and the rest of society. You don't have to create a huge corporation that will suck up all your time for the rest of your life. I recommend a path that allows you to stay mobile and to have a less stressful way to survive in any economy.

Don't get me wrong: if you start a small business that becomes hugely successful, you can run with it, but know that it will require tremendous time and energy with less time to play. In truth, each business I started was with the idea of doing as little work as possible while maximizing my leisure time. In every case, I had an exit plan for getting out with as little effort and as much money as possible. I did not want to be tied down to a desk, a labor contract, or any other device that restricted my freedom.

A startup should have a long-term vision. A key message in all your dealings with clients, suppliers, and even your staff should be that the business is going to be around for the long run.

However, although the business should be long-term, my involvement doesn't have to be. I like creating an entity, running it for a while, and then moving on while leaving the business in other capable hands.

Many icemen (Independent Creative Entrepreneurs) establish a series of startups, as I did, and truly enjoy their lives. These folks have learned to adapt to almost any economic situation. In some cases, they have done it with little or no formal business training. Whether it is intuitive or a sheer matter of survival, they just do it.

I actually don't like business, especially big business. I don't like what it sometimes represents. Picture a giant vacuum nozzle, hovering over our wallets and bank accounts, sucking up our last pennies. The businesses that make money without providing value have turned many consumers off. Many potential entrepreneurs have decided not to start a business because of the negative view they have of commerce.

In reality, I honestly don't even like some of the day-to-day tasks of running a small business. I don't like negotiating, I don't like babysitting a staff, I don't like confrontation, and I don't like the idea that I always have to be on my toes because some other businessperson may outsmart me.

However, I am an idea man and love to create something of value. If I have what you want and you deem the price for my services or product fair, we do the deal with no mess, no fuss, and no pain. Of course, this is all fantasy. You need some business acumen; without it, someone who thinks business should be win-lose (they win and you lose) will swallow you whole.

I admit I have had my share of frustrations and satisfaction with both small and large corporations. As consumers we are more likely to feel a loss of control when we deal with big business rather than small companies. That may explain why most Americans look favorably upon small business and less favorably upon large business.

According to the 2012 Public Affairs Pulse Survey, 53 percent of Americans have a highly favorable opinion of small businesses, while only 16 percent of the respondents say the same for major corporations.
This is a steady trend. More people see small business

as an extension of an unwritten social contract, one in which society expects morals and ethics to be held in high regard when conducting trade. When more people recognize their talents, get over their fears, take control, and believe they can create and contribute something of value without destroying the moral commitment we have with one another, more will get on the small-business bandwagon.

According to the Small Business Association (SBA), the number of small businesses continues to grow, accounting for 54 percent of sales in the U.S., 55 percent of all jobs in the U.S., and up to 66 percent of all new jobs created since the 1970s.

3. Foreign Horizons

*"The two most important requirements for major
success: are first being in the right place at the right
time, and second, doing something about it."*
- Ray Kroc

I am writing this book from somewhere in Europe. If
you have ever dreamed of living in a foreign country,
my life can be seen as the ultimate example of what
one can achieve as an iceman. We all have dreams. Just
ask a friend or a complete stranger, "Where would you
be if you had your druthers?" The likely response
would not be where you were asking the question, but
somewhere else such as a distant country or an island
paradise. Yep, most of us want out, to a place we might
have read about or heard about.

I left the U.S. for several reasons; the key reason was
the loss of my main business in New York after 9/11. I
had no idea what to do. However, with my history of
establishing and running small businesses (always with
control and flexibility in mind), I considered all
options, even setting up a business in Europe.

The seed for this move was planted many years before.
In 1998, a friend and I were invited to Barcelona to
assist a musician friend on a concert tour. During the
trip, we began to think about Europe as the place to

live and even retire.

A week after the 9/11 disasters, I was sitting in my office in complete silence when the phone suddenly rang. It was a call from Europe from my musician friend. What a surprise. He inquired about my family and then proceeded to ask how business was. What business? The silence, as they say, was deafening. I lost many of my clients to the disaster. He reminded me of an idea I had on that wonderful trip to Barcelona. The idea was to open a seaside bar. It didn't take long to set the wheels in motion. I immediately instructed my secretary to purchase airline tickets for me to scout for a suitable location with my friend.

Several trips later and after checking in with family and friends, I found myself moving to Europe as the proud owner of a bar. The speed in which this happened was unbelievable. The established regulatory maze was enough to discourage any sane entrepreneur. The locals later told me that we were lucky: opening so quickly was the exception. Nevertheless it was done, and I now had an income for survival in my new environment.

Indeed, opening a business in Europe was crazy because of the normal bureaucracy one faces when attempting this, and because of the general attitude about starting your own business in Europe. Most Europeans I've talked to aren't interested in opening their own business. In Europe, there is a strong tendency to rely on government jobs or to work reluctantly for a company for low wages with little chance of getting promoted. In reality, only a limited number of opportunities exist, along with a particular cultural malaise when it comes to Europeans starting their own business.

What is also true is many Europeans seek a lifestyle that lets them "work to live" rather than "live to work." Many Americans do the opposite of Europeans, creating a life that is out of balance. I try to show people that with your own business, you can achieve the delicate balance between work and play. It's one of the keys to a full life.

It's sometimes easy to forget that drive and ambition aren't the only things that set Americans apart. Americans also have the desire to create or produce something of value, something that solves a problem or enhances people's lives.

Ironically Europeans, like the rest of the world, now want a piece of that entrepreneurial action and the freedom it brings.

As an American, you start out as a member of the "entrepreneur club." As a European or World Citizen, you have an open invitation. However, regardless of where you grew up, it is still necessary to capture the spirit and put it to use. Remember, if you keep getting invited to the party and don't show up, the invitations will stop.

In America, we have the advantage of more opportunities, and most of us are taught that you can accomplish anything including starting your own business. Those small businesses are developed within a free enterprise environment with some of the least regulations. Yet some still don't take advantage of this because of fear or other factors.

Take a look at this chart.

Economy	Ease of Doing Business Rank ▲	Starting a Business	Registering Property	Getting Credit	Trading Across Borders
Singapore	1	10	17	19	41
New Zealand	2	1	1	1	55
Denmark	3	29	9	28	1
Korea, Rep.	4	23	40	42	31
Hong Kong SAR, China	5	4	59	19	47
United Kingdom	6	17	45	19	38
United States *	7	49	34	2	34
Sweden	8	16	11	70	17
Norway	9	24	13	70	45
Finland	10	33	20	42	32
Taiwan, China	11	22	18	59	65
Macedonia, FYR	12	2	50	42	26
Australia	13	11	47	5	89
Canada	14	3	42	7	44
Germany	15	107	62	28	35

Estonia	16	15	4	28	24
Ireland	17	25	39	28	48
Malaysia	18	14	38	28	49
Iceland	19	40	15	59	64
Lithuania	20	8	2	28	19

The countries listed above are the Top 20 based on ease of doing business. The rankings for all of the world economies are benchmarked to 2015. Notice that only ten of Europe's fifty countries are in the top 20, which makes what we did with the bar all the more remarkable. Interestingly, if you look at the specific categories on the chart, you will see that, post-startup, it can be easier to conduct business in the listed European countries than in other countries. You can also see that although the United States is number 7 for ease overall, it didn't crack the top 10 in the specific category of 'Starting a Business.' The U.S. is at 49 in this category, which is still good relative to most other countries. The rankings were influenced by other factors like getting construction permits, hooking up electricity, enforcing contracts and resolving insolvency.

The point of sharing this information is to get you to expand your horizons and use your noodle and initiative to START a business, any business, anywhere. Opportunities exist everywhere. If you feel stuck and have dreamed about starting a business . . . start thinking globally. Don't let fear rule your life.

Plenty of opportunities exist. If you are hardwired with a sense of freedom and entrepreneurial spirit, the challenges become easier to overcome.

From personal experience, I know that the old saying that "the grass is greener on the other side," is true for me. Working for the man and putting your hope into buying lottery tickets is the wrong path. Your chances are much better when you start your own gig.

4. The Real Road to Freedom: Passive Income

"The only thing money gives you is the freedom of not worrying about money."
- Johnny Carson

What truly makes my entrepreneurship work is my ability to create small companies that spin off earnings. This meets part of the definition of passive income; however, the other more significant part is that I can receive income while no longer having direct involvement in an entity.

For an extreme example of how passive income works, take a look at Mitt Romney's tax returns (if you can). The man is an icon when it comes to this. His picture should be next to the term 'passive income' in the dictionary. I am being sarcastic; nevertheless, the biggest secret to his wealth is the use of entities that spin off passive income.

Anyone who receives rental payments, royalties, dividends, or pension funds is receiving passive income. What may be new to some of you is that you can do this with a small business. You just need to structure the business so that when you either leave as an owner/manager or sell the business; you can generate years of potentially tax-free or minimally taxed income.

My advice for you icemen is to check with your accountant as to how best set up the business: Ask how to structure the loans, classify initial capital investment, take depreciation for equipment, and use other methods to reduce your tax bite and allow you the benefits of passive income. These techniques are not just available to the rich; they can be used by anyone going into business for themselves. If your accountant smirks, laughs, or seems ignorant about this stuff . . . find a different accountant.

This is more or less the common theme among all the businesses I created. I always discussed the benefits of each startup and the exit plan with a professional.

When selling some of the businesses, I worked out a deal where the payments were made over a five- to seven-year period.

Most people prefer to get paid all the money upon selling; however, the best solution is to get the buyer to commit to the transaction with a substantial deposit and to take the rest as delayed, passive income. This structure is especially ideal if this creates a minimum tax bite. Sometimes it can be a little risky, but if you sell or leave the business in safe hands you may find this fairly easy.

Also, when selling a business, make sure you have the ability to get it back upon default. The chances of a default happening are nil and slim. I have given private mortgages over a seven-year term and taken notes from buyers for a period of up to five years. I never had a problem. In the case with the mortgage, I was able to finance one of my businesses. With the note from another buyer, I traveled Europe and set up a new business in a foreign country. Always think about the easiest thing to do to be free and maintain your independence.

Having a steady income over an extended period of time puts your mind at ease and allows you to think of new business ideas and even to finance them from the passive income. Of course, the other tremendous advantage is the flexibility to do nothing!

After running each business for a few years, I sold it and moved on to the next business. The one exception was my main business, headhunting, which remained central to generating a steady revenue stream. That income stream allowed me to travel or do what I wanted. The businesses that I started all had a built-in system for providing an income stream. For example, in my recruiting and consulting business, the information technology workers placed on projects were contracted for the life of the projects and the company continued to pay for as long as the person was on 'billing.'

Starting a business that can give you a passive income stream affords you plenty of leeway if you decide to take off. All you need is a competent secretary to see to it that the invoices are sent and paid in a timely fashion. For businesses requiring daily supervision, I employed competent managers so that I could enjoy the flexibility of functioning as a silent partner.

Of the 11 businesses outlined in this book, I had to be there on a day-to-day basis for only three of them, including my first business, which was in retail. I was the sole owner, and I had to do everything from buying to merchandising and selling. All of the entities I still control generate a healthy income with remarkably little effort on my part. This includes owning an eBay store, writing how-to EBooks, and being a partner in an English academy.

The English school generates an income from teachers on billing (similar to the IT consulting) and allows me to farm myself out as an independent consultant, giving me fantastic freedom as I can choose the clients and the times I want to work. The money is decent and the time well spent and enjoyable. Moreover, the teaching schedule calls for a sabbatical during the summer, which allows me time to write and do other things for pure pleasure.

So the idea is to aim for total flexibility in any business you start. Before you decide on the business, examine the method for receiving payments and the potential for that business to spin off a future income stream. After my first endeavor with retail, I gravitated toward businesses that could spin off residual income. Unless you can fully retire with a decent pension, this may be your best method for gaining your freedom.

The following information is essential. The structure

E.J.Kelly

you choose for your startup will affect not only your present income, but also your income when you decide to exit or sell the business. In some cases, you can start with one structure and subsequently choose a different one down the road. In some situations, this will save tons of money.

For example, if your business is based in the United States, ask your accountant or attorney whether the business could change from a C corporation to an S corporation. Or ask about the reverse. Could your business start out as a partnership and change into an LLC? (See below for an explanation of different business structures.) The timing for changing the structure of your entity can be crucial. However, you should thoroughly consult and consider before you take action; just make the professional you consult is qualified to advise you about business entities and make sure they know your goal of eventually having passive income.

Business Structures:

Current I.R.S.-approved business structures in the United States:

Sole proprietorship: Essentially this allows anyone to establish a business without forming a corporation or a limited liability company. For a retail business, a sole proprietorship was all I needed to get a license to buy and sell wholesale goods. While a sole proprietorship can cost little or nothing to set up, you are personally liable for all taxes and debt of the business, so consider buying some type of business insurance to protect yourself.

Partnerships: Two or more individuals can contribute to a startup by contributing money, property, labor, or other valuables. The actual entity pays no income tax; however, partners are taxed as individuals for any profits or gains received. As with sole proprietorships, your personal protection from creditors or anyone wanting to sue you is limited with this type of entity, although that exposure varies depending on the type of partnership you choose. You should consider buying business or even personal liability insurance.

Corporations: If you use this structure, the IRS and lenders will treat your business as an entity separate from you as an individual as long as you treat it that way yourself. However, in order for a corporation to obtain credit, one or more of the stockholders (owners) will likely be required to sign a personal guaranty for a loan. When a corporation is formed, shares are distributed to those that contribute money, property, or other valuables.

As of this writing, two types of corporations exist in the U.S., C corporations and S corporations. You should discuss the advantages and disadvantages of each type of entity with a professional. The main difference relates to federal taxation: an 'S' corporation allows the income, losses, and deductions of the corporation to be passed to the shareholders, whereas the profits of a C corporation are taxed to the corporation when earned and taxed to the shareholders when distributed as dividends. This creates a double tax. When a corporation distributes dividends to shareholders, it cannot deduct those dividends as an expense, and shareholders cannot deduct any corporate losses on their personal taxes.

Again, as long as you, the owner, treat the corporation as a separate entity, then you, as an owner, can limit your personal liability. (There are additional requirements to consider if you are also a director or officer in the corporation.)

LLCs: This type of entity is becoming popular because it combines the best attributes of a partnership and a corporation. As with a partnership, management is flexible and taxes are passed through, so that there isn't double taxation on the same profits. As with a corporation, LLCs are considered entities separate from their owners, so that owners can enjoy limited liability. Most LLCs have at least two members; however, some states will allow you to set up an LLC with only one member . . . you. For more information on this topic, I highly recommend you visit the delightful IRS website.

5. Working for the 'Man' Sucks

"Unfortunately most ways of making big money take a long time.
By the time one has made the money one is too old to enjoy it."
- Ian Fleming,

Working for the man may suck, but you have to start somewhere. Work for a boss and learn something. That something is different from what you learned at any university or college. A formal education is commendable; however, learning to function in a productive environment is more valuable. Education will lead you to more intellectual pursuits and enrich your life, but it may not do you any good in the real business world. Some of the material, quite frankly, is useless. Will studying history, philosophy, music, or literature help you achieve freedom? If true freedom and survival lie in being able to produce or develop something of value, you are better off learning about this stuff on the job. An apprentice learns more than a student about what it takes to earn and be productive in the real world.

Working for the man will give you the opportunity to pick up a trade, as they say, or to learn a valuable discipline, such as recruiting and selling, two skills that have helped me repeatedly. Once you have learned a discipline, you have something to fall back on. Moreover, you will learn organizational methods and various systems for bringing your product or service to the market. Working as an employee exposes you to different ideas and can help motivate you to start your own business.

I suggest you start your search by picking a growing sector or field where specific knowledge is required to generate money. Find one you feel comfortable with because normally you will be employed for a considerable amount of time.

Once engaged, make every effort to form a good relationship with the owner or trainer, who can become your ongoing mentor. During this experience, you must try to understand the business from nuance to substance. Determine what attributes the boss or manager possesses. Notice how that person manages time, prioritizes tasks, communicates with staff and customers, and meets goals. This is the real world, and it is a true learning laboratory to prepare you as a future entrepreneur.

Don't underestimate this approach. As you will see, I was able to parlay a single discipline into several startups. This one discipline or area of concentration allowed me to be whimsical and gave me the confidence to say, "If all else fails, I can always get a job."

Indeed, working for the man sucks . . . except that it provides you with money and skills to help you survive. The path that most will take on the journey from survival to freedom involves putting in time as an employee. Travel well and learn well along that path.

In the next section, I describe each job I held and the lessons I learned from it that you could apply to your own startup.

6. "Five Pre-Occupations"

Preoccupation: A subject or matter that engrosses someone:
"Their main preoccupation was how to feed their families."
Occupation: a job or profession.

This chapter title actually makes a great deal of sense. Indeed, along the journey, preoccupation always existed as well as the need to get a gig. The use of the word 'preoccupation' also accurately describes my desire during that journey to start my own business, to use this 'pre-' period to prepare myself for the rest of my life.

A. Midway Magic

For my first job at seventeen, 'the man' hired me on a whim. The job was running a midway kiosk in an amusement park.

'The Man' in this case was an outstanding businessman and human being. He taught me things I still remember. He taught me more than any college professor or expert in any future business I would get involved in. The three basic things he passed on were:

✓ Give your client the respect that you expect in return.
✓ Give them the benefit of the doubt and be prepared to go the extra mile.
✓ Learn to read the emotional signals they cast off.

The ability to understand people and determine their motives or needs is essential to being successful in any business. Information on this topic is plentiful, so I won't go into all the specifics here, since I want to focus on information you may not be able to find other places. The basics are to ask direct questions, stop, listen, listen, and listen more and react accordingly. Your goal is to determine the motivation of your client.

The rest of the equation calls for you to observe their body language. Certain physical moves may have specific meanings. If you don't know about body language, plenty of information exists on this topic as well, and it behooves you as an iceman to learn the basics. Most of us have this ability, but we don't put it to use. It lies dormant until we suddenly realize it is necessary to make a living.

In the 'midway' as we called it, the job called for me to extract as much money as possible from the customer. The word 'extract' is used tongue-in-cheek because ostensibly we were part of the overall entertainment provided by the park. So I would stand inside the kiosk yelling at the top of my lungs, " Get one in and win" or "Come play with me," anything to get the customer over to the stand.

The best 'marks' were groups or couples. They would hear me and look at the kiosk stacked to the hilt with stuffed animals, and then come over. I gave them a gigantic smile as I quickly sized them up. Within seconds, by sheer observation, I usually could determine what kind of money they had and their motives. I noticed the clothes and the kind of watch they were wearing. The second part of the process involved asking questions: "Are you having a good time?" "Did you win anything yet?" "Are you here by yourself?"

With a couple, the number one motivation of the guy was to win the 'big one' for his girlfriend. With groups, the motivation often was to have fun and stroke the ego. Armed with this information, with a bit of prodding, I could get many of them, like magic, to deposit lots of money in my apron. In the case of couples, I continually asked the girlfriend, while pointing to the jumbo stuffed elephants, "Do you want the 'big one.' This was a subtle use of sex that worked like a charm. I was flabbergasted to see the extremes to which men would go to win the 'big one.' In several instances, the player would try to buy the damn elephant directly. I would say, "Sir, it is against the rules to sell this to you. You must win it."

A co-worker who was my second midway mentor worked for the 'man' for several years. He ran a different game and was not so subtle with the sex thing. Each night he would come to work with the intent of 'playing the field.' This guy keyed in on women.

Sometimes, after draining them of their money, he would disappear. I couldn't figure this out until the time I noticed a seismic shift in the stuffed animals. On his breaks he was shagging in the back of his kiosk. This guy was making big money and making it big with the ladies. He understood body language better than anyone else and, for me, forever changed the meaning of "Get one in, and you win."

However, this midway Romeo's skill eventually failed him. One night a huge fight broke out in front of his stand. Sure enough, the guy had hit on the wrong woman. He later altered his game, tempered his pitch, and stuck to stuffing his apron with big bucks.

These early lessons in human behavior and how to sell to it are still helping me today.

The 'man' in this case tapped my knack for understanding people by guiding me gingerly in the many ways of selling to the public. He spent hours training me, showing he trusted me and giving me an immense amount of responsibility, all the while boosting my confidence. After the training period and minimal experience, I had the ability to understand people and their motivations. I was ultimately quite successful in getting them to spend buckets of money.

This was seasonal work and probably established my ideas about balancing work with freedom. The season ran from March to October every year. Ideally, a seasonal worker tries to make as much money as possible and spends the other months at leisure. In the final month of my first season, a girlfriend suggested we go to Puerto Rico. Nice suggestion. At six in the morning, we hopped over to the airport, bought tickets, and flew to the Caribbean for a three-month stay. I could take a long vacation because I had the flexibility and the money, along with confidence from knowing the job would be waiting for me when I returned.

Takeaways and thoughts:

✓ Training is critical. If at all possible, get it straight from the top, from the owner or the manager.

✓ Learn to observe, qualify, and understand what motivates the client; learn to listen, listen, and listen some more. The first step in selling is to gather information.

✓ Be smart about displaying your merchandise; those jumbo elephants were so enticing that everyone wanted one.

✓ Finally, try to keep your sexual urges away from the office!

B. Restaurant Rage

The shortest and most forgettable job I held was working for a gourmet burger restaurant in Wall Street. The reason I needed this gig was because I gone back to school to get a degree in fashion and was desperately seeking a job with flexible hours to support myself. I should have known terrible things were on the horizon when the interviewer asked me no questions about my related experience. The restaurant needed a body. After memorizing the short menu over the weekend, I was put to work serving tables that Monday with no training.

Upon arriving, I was handed an apron and assigned to Section 8. (There is a section 8 in the unemployment office which helped burn this number into my head.) Anyway, the section in question had four tables and was situated away from the scenic windows of Wall Street. In short, it was the worst area to work as a waiter. That Monday, I had three groups for lunch and garnered $8 in tips. I was both depressed and happy: I was happy because I didn't make any mistakes. My rosy vision of Wall Street fat cats melted away as I pocketed their tightwad tips. After lunch, a fellow server asked how it went. I told her, and she said, "Things will get better." The next day was pretty much the same. However, I made $12 and was feeling much better about the job and the potential for increasing my tips.

And then it happened. On Thursday, a server called in sick, and I was sent to the hectic section near the windows. What a disaster! Plates tipped over, trays fell, and I never used the word 'sorry' so many times in one afternoon. All the while, the manager—'the man'— watched with a stoic expression and didn't lift a finger to help. It got worse after the lunch crowd left, the manager called a meeting. With seven servers and the rest of the staff in attendance, he began the meeting by asking, "Why are the ketchup bottles empty?" What? We looked at each other in total disbelief and bewilderment. I honestly didn't know who was responsible for filling the ketchup bottles. Then the manager began to screech as if a hot iron had poked him. He screamed about being professional, about being careful, and about losing one's composure when serving the customer. This of course was directed at me. Generally, I take criticism well and let it slide, but there was more. He said I was to stay an extra hour to fill all the ketchup and mustard bottles. I was to fill those suckers immediately.

That did it. I was done. I called him an asshole and walked out.

These are some of the lessons I learned in this brief job:

> ✓ Never chastise an employee in front of other staff. That is unprofessional behavior that demoralizes employees.
> ✓ When you hire someone, make sure that person is trained and informed of the job's responsibilities. It's a good idea to write those duties down in a manual. If an employee isn't trained properly, don't blame the employee entirely.
> ✓ Being a waiter is a really hard job, harder than most people realize. Being professional, courteous, and efficient while serving hungry and demanding customers requires a juggling act. So the next time you and yours find yourself in a restaurant, give your server some respect and a big tip.

C. Five Suits and a Wedding.

The third full-time position was working in a store selling suits. The store, a former warehouse, was huge, with the sales area on the first floor and a storage room on the second floor. I was hired on the spot after explaining my experience of selling fashion accessories directly to the public. In addition, I told them I was a clothes horse. In truth, I had one ratty jacket, one soup-stained tie, and two pairs of decrepit slacks. In those days, the sole motivation for working in a clothing store was to replenish one's wardrobe with the discounts the store offered its employees. There's no need to tell you where most of my first paycheck went.

Anyway, let me jog your memory a little. The key marketing and selling point for this so-called suit wholesaler was a 'free TV.' Do you remember the days when retailers and banks would throw in a gift when you bought from them? This was one of them. If you bought $500 worth of merchandise, you would get a free television.

No catch, except that the suits were horrible. We had plaid polyester suits; we had pinstriped polyester suits. We had pants and mismatched jackets made of, you guessed it, polyester. We had DuPont Qiana shirts and ties; do you remember disco? On the rack, nicely pressed, the suits looked gorgeous. These were everything a well-dressed man could want. The average price tag for a suit was $249. Therefore, if a customer bought two suits and spent another two bucks, or bought one suit with additional pants and accessories, he could, theoretically, leave with a free television.

This enticement worked well for the business, because the wholesale price for the suits was only $34. Some three-piece suits cost a bit more, but even they were cheaply made. As salesmen, we had the authority to negotiate and lower the price of each item relative to the resistance we got from customers, as long as we charged at least double the wholesale cost. During training, we had been given instructions on how to sell, sell, and sell. With the first round of resistance, we offered the customer 10 percent off; with the next whiff of resistance, we offered an additional 10 percent off. With the discounts, few customers bought enough to get the free television.

I worked with quite a few characters at the store. One of my favorites was a salesman named Chuck. Chuck was stout and fleshy, but he always managed to squeeze into one of the store's three-piece specials with the vest left unbuttoned. You could always tell he was around because a clucking sound preceded him; he had an ill-fitting plastic cap on a front tooth that he repeatedly sucked on. Chuck also had a way with words. His most famous saying: "Don't hurt nobody."

He said this when you arrived at work and left work. He greeted and said good-bye to customers with the saying. On payday, when receiving his huge commission check, he would loudly say this to the payroll clerk, so we all could hear. It got to the point that on my way to the bathroom, my most pressing thoughts were replaced by this innocuous double negative.

This guy was the best salesman I have ever met. Within minutes he had the customer in tears from laughter and knew their entire history. He once outfitted an entire wedding party, promising the suits would be tailored and pressed (no need for ironing as these beauties were already stiff) well before the wedding day. I would see him walking over to the cashier with a customer who was buying five suits, a couple of ties, belts, and some trousers. Chuck talked the guy into buying five similar suits for $75 each, and the rest was gravy. But at the end of the negotiation, the poor customer hadn't spent enough to get a free TV. Nevertheless, the customer was satisfied. "Hey, Chuck, did you hurt him?" "No, the guy has a new wardrobe and is happy as a lark."

My work at this clothing store lasted about fourteen months. And then it happened. I walked to work one morning and found 'going out of business' signs on the windows. My first thought was that this was a new strategy to get more people through the door. It wasn't. Within the month, we were all gone.

The public wanted more than just free TVs. They wanted stylish, quality clothing. Management didn't see this coming. The wholesalers were bleeding red ink and stopped producing these sartorial splendors. We had no more $34 suits to sell. The public's taste had totally changed. In the fashion industry, this happens all the time.

What was so strange was that, months earlier, the staff

had seen the writing on the wall, but when we had taken our concerns to the managers, they did little to change the situation. At one point, when it was too late to save a sinking ship, management began seeking new, high-end suppliers, but few were willing to sell to a store with a reputation for handing out free TVs. Upscale suppliers wanted no association with this form of hyped-up retailing. Come to think of it, where had they been getting those $34 suits? Perhaps they fell off a truck.

Over the next few weeks, we sold most things at a little above cost. With the store closure on the horizon, I began my search for a new gig, but I soon realized this game wasn't for me. I took my last commission check and went on a long holiday to the French Caribbean.

Here are some of the things I learned from this position:

✓ First and foremost, always sell a quality product or service.
✓ Merchandizing tactics such as free TVs do work. The giveaway created buzz and a great deal of foot traffic.
✓ Again, I saw that a well-thought-out training program is essential for any business.
✓ A generous commission plan is an essential motivator for salespeople.
✓ Staying abreast of trends, especially in the fashion industry, is a must.
✓ Diversifying the lines of merchandise is essential.

✓ And finally, "Don't hurt nobody."

D. A Workman's Agency

The fourth position in my short list of full-time jobs happened after a long vacation. Refreshed and invigorated, I began thinking about setting up a business, but I was having trouble deciding on the type of business. The default was to go back to the streets and start hustling again with my mini-kiosk, which I describe in my retailing chapter. Just as I decided to return to entrepreneurship, two things happened to delay another round of self-employment. Before leaving for the islands, I had had several interviews with some upscale retailers. The thinking was if I could sell plastic to the public, I could sell quality stuff in my sleep.

An offer arrived from Barney's men's clothing. Before I could accept it, a friend of a friend called me out of the blue, inquiring about my next move. This person knew something about my background and was recruiting for a job he had within the Information Technology sector. It sounded intriguing.

With an offer in hand from Barney's and nothing to lose, I agreed to meet him. The meeting went well, although I had no idea what the hell he was talking about. Something about recruiting IT professionals for fees. The idea of getting paid by companies for finding employees for them was strange to me. Yet it was true. We had a second meeting, and he extended an offer to me that included an intensive four-month training program with a basic salary plus commissions. This was going to be tough: a real challenge. I knew positively nothing about the industry. However, I was attracted by the chance to learn something new so that I could get away from retail.

What's wrong with retail? Glad you asked. Three big drawbacks exist: the hours are grueling; retail lacks potential for passive income, and working retail means working with the general public, which sometimes represents one version of hell.

The fourth month into the hands-on training, I made my first direct deal, earning a $24,000 fee for the firm, which I was told was the biggest in company history. The firm charged the hiring companies as much as 30 percent of a placement's first-year salary; the recruiter received from 10 to 50 percent of that fee, depending on experience. This was so far removed from anything I had ever attempted before.

Learning the process and the technical terms were like learning a new language, the training was intense, and the idea of working with clients without meeting them was disconcerting. All the work was done via the phone. "Smile and dial," as they say. Lack of face time was okay for working with clients, but we always met face-to-face with candidates. In all cases, we were instructed to bring the candidate into the office for a technical interview and a visual. This rule generally applied to new candidates. However, there was this one time when I made a classic rookie mistake.

Getting off the phone with an order to fill a 'hot job,' I

immediately scoured the database for a qualified applicant. Bingo, I found one within minutes. The interview was scheduled for the following week. I called the candidate several times to prepare him and to give him all the necessary information about the job. Several days went by with no word from the client. Nervously, I put a call into the client. The first words out of his mouth were, "Did you ever meet this guy?" I said, "Honestly, never, although he was in our database." I had assumed that someone else in the office had met the guy. Well, what do you know, this 'technical executive' showed up in a tattered, checkered, three-piece polyester suit.

All that was missing was the free TV. Embarrassing!

Later, I was told that even seasoned recruiters make mistakes. There was the classic case of a qualified candidate meeting all the internal and client requirements only to show up on the start date with a totally shaved head and a hoop earring. It cost the company a fee of $16,000.

This stuff is real...it happens! On the brighter side, over the succeeding months, little old me generated close to $250,000 dollars in fees for the company.

During the first two years I worked for this company, a shift took place within the industry. Big companies began hiring consultants. Management at my company took notice of this and quickly set out to support these new companies. This led to our firm establishing relationships with a new set of clients: IT Consulting

Companies. I was selected to head up this new division.

I was promoted to management level, providing professionals to consulting firms. This was pretty cool for a rookie and for someone with no previous management experience. This continued for almost another two years, to the point where my boss as a bonus leased a car for me. I didn't need it. I was living in Manhattan where the garage cost more than my monthly apartment rent.

Honestly, I stepped into a hot market. Companies were going crazy to fill IT positions; as a result, some of them gave us exclusives and offered higher fees. Over the two years, I continued to learn as much about the business as I could and managed to save quite a few bucks, all while envisioning doing this business on my own.

And, eventually, it happened. (See chapter on headhunting)

Takeaways:

> ✓ Don't let your brain slip into autopilot when securing a full-time position. Think it through. Go for something that is ridiculously foreign. Something that in the short term will be a real challenge can pay enormous rewards later.
> ✓ Learn a discipline. Learn the internal systems that make the company successful.
> ✓ Be willing to step up to any and all continued challenges within the company.

Show some initiative, and you may be rewarded with further training or a promotion.

E. Selling Advice

The fifth and final position of my illustrious employment career came as a direct result of working for the above company. One of our clients, a recruiter, recruited me. The consulting firm thought I would make a terrific salesman, selling IT services to its clients.

If this all sounds confusing, it wasn't, I assure you. The entire industry was completely vertical, and most people knew each other. If you enjoyed a strong reputation in one area of the business, you could be slotted into a different position easily. My reputation as a recruiter and my knowledge of the industry led the new company to go after me. Besides, at this point, I was looking for a new challenge, and the company made me an offer I couldn't refuse.

They assigned me to a mentor, a seasoned salesman making an amazing amount of money. When he showed me his commissions check once, my jaw dropped. Who knew? He was raking in $23,000 a month.

This company provided consultants for assignments or projects. My mentor had an account with a large communications company that was being dismantled. His success came from his uncanny ability to identify problems within organizations.

In this case, he realized that this company had no idea where its equipment was and what liability it would have for that equipment after the breakup.

He wrote a letter to the company's head honcho, who set off bells, whistles, and anything else that resembled an alarm. So many emails flew around that the internal system crashed. Managers were called on the carpet, off the carpet, and later a few were found buried under the carpet. I'm just joking here, but this astonishing problem was huge. This was big money we were talking about, and not one executive had considered it.

The salesman, my mentor, was introduced to district managers and their subordinates. Within six months, he had 40 consultants working on different projects that generated about $600,000 per month for our company. (See startups below.)

My mentor at this company wasn't exceptionally talented, but he was able to see the bigger picture of a company's organization, needs, and problems. When he sold, he presented himself and the company as problem solvers. His whole approach became what we called a 'consulting sale': Identify a problem and create an environment where the company becomes a vital part of the solution. The problem is solved when both sides jointly attack it.

The approach was fantastic, as it allowed for immediate credibility. The sale could be closed quickly, and negotiating for rates became almost an afterthought. The man's reputation, as they say, preceded him. On the many days when I listened to his prospecting calls, I learned that most clients knew about him and even anticipated his call.

Boy, did I luck out. I was assigned to a great trainer. Three months in, I had 15 people on billing and was enjoying a fair amount of success. My experience in recruiting was a tremendous help as finding the right people was still a serious problem. So recruiting the people needed for open assignments became part of my work. This, as you may have guessed, required a lot of time and effort.

All was well until life interceded: my wife was experiencing a difficult pregnancy. I needed to be close to home. Decision time . . . traveling to the various clients had to come to an end. Management, after being made aware of my problem, decided to bring me 'in house' to do the recruiting for all the company's salespeople. Since this was my specialty, it was a great solution.

The takeaways from this position:

> ✓ Learn how to identify a problem at the client's business and then present a solution.
> ✓ Include consultancy in your sales effort to increase your chances of closing the deal.
> ✓ Remain flexible with employees. This was a valuable lesson that I applied to all my future businesses.

7. What Business Plan...You Need A Personal Plan

"Many people spend more time in planning the wedding than they do in planning the marriage".
- Zig Ziglar

One of the pieces of advice people planning a startup will hear most often is: You need a business plan. I never wrote a formal business plan for any of the startups in this book; I never needed to. The businesses I started were directly related to research, work, and training I received from full-time jobs in my "pre-occupations."

If you are employed in a business that enjoys being in a growing, functioning sector that is making tons of money, the only thing you need is the desire to do it for yourself. If you were trained well and paid attention while you were employed, you know the internal systems, the organizational structure, and the marketing that will make your new startup a success. You already know the competition. In theory, you also have a base of clients who know you and your reputation. Management skills should be learned and tested at those full-time jobs.

All of the aforementioned are some of the main components in a business plan. The one component that is missing is funding. Even for this you don't require a formal plan unless you need the money from an outside source. After I established one main line of business, I rarely needed funding for new opportunities because I kept a low overhead and contributed at least 10 percent of my salary and all profits to a "Take This Job and Shove It Fund." I tapped this SIF for new ventures.

I needed a formal plan only two times. Once was to fund a payroll and the other was to convince a crazy landlord that I had enough business experience and knew what I was doing. In both cases, my accountants developed the plans, and I paid dearly. The cost of the reports was irrelevant, though, because considerable money was coming in and cash flow was excellent. The reports were professional and did the job. Use your resources when you need them.

Interestingly, approval of the line of credit for payroll (see consulting below) was based on my knowledge of the industry and asset financing from my main business (recruiting). More funding details are provided at the end of each startup section below.

It's ironic that most people still recommend going to the banks or the government to finance their startup. It is also a myth that the U.S. Small Business Association is a lender. Wrong! Banks provide the funding for loans; the SBA only guarantees them. In reality, the bank makes the decision about your funding. , Getting startup funds from any bank is exceedingly difficult. According to an article from 'Yahoo Small Business

Advisor' dated March 30, 2012, banks are rejecting up to 90 percent of all small business loan applications.

Banks are notorious for rejecting loans for new businesses. They want company history and strong financials. However, if you're trying to fund a startup, your company has no track record or collateral to support the loan. Moreover, if your personal credit isn't sterling, the banks will use this as a further excuse for turning you down. You will spend money and time developing a formal plan and financial package only to be denied a loan.

My advice is to keep the money you would spend on developing the plan and use it for other needs of the business. Unless you were born on 'third base' or have some collateral, you are unlikely to get a loan for your business. If you do get lucky, read all the documents to make sure you aren't tethered to the mother ship (bank) for the rest of your life.

If security is required, use it carefully and stay away from pledging personal assets such as your house, your pension, or your children. As an Iceman, I want no part of risking assets needed by my family.

So the plan you need is a personal one of self-reflection. Ask yourself major questions: Do you truly want your freedom? Do you want to work for someone else? Do you want to be well compensated for the time and energy you put into a project? Are you willing to sacrifice in the short term for long-term results? Most important: Is the business you selected going to spin off income, and is it the right business for you? (Why in the world would you get involved with something you don't like?)

Also ask yourself minor questions: Do you like to travel? Do you like being told what to wear to work? Do you have the energy to do this? Do you have the talent? Can you find the resources to assist you in your endeavors? The answers to these and similar questions should be used as part of your informal plan. Be honest with yourself. If your answers to the above questions indicate you are suited to independence and entrepreneurship, look forward . . . and get in the game. Now to ease your nerves a little, I will remind you that you can always get a JOB!

And for those of you more inclined to be pragmatic, the following is a template of both an informal and formal plan for business.

The first is the informal approach, which at a minimum should be incorporated into your personal plan. Below I list the reasons most businesses fail, based on an abstract called "Using Goldratt's Thinking Process to Improve the Success Rate of Small Business Start-ups." I follow each failure reason with suggestions for preventing or overcoming it. In your own planning, figure out ways to prevent these problems from sinking your startup. Personally, I believe most business failures result from an inability to set and achieve goals and handle challenges. Assess yourself: Have you set measurable goals that are in tune with your character and values? When the going gets tough, do you quit or do you work even harder to make success yours?

Reasons for business failures and my advice for overcoming these obstacles:

1. Insufficient Operating Capital.

A. Yes, this number one reason for failure can be a big obstacle. However, if you follow my advice and create a SIF (Shove It Fund, remember?), you will have savings to get any new business off the ground. This also lets you have a smaller operating budget because you're not paying off a loan. Once you have your core business established, one that will give you passive income, as a last resort in launching another startup, you can provide a financial plan to the banks that offers your main business as collateral so that you can borrow to fund the new venture.

2. Lack Of Realistic Planning.

A. As I said above, you really should have a plan, but the plan is based on your experiences with other businesses, either as employee or owner. Because you generally will be jumping into a similar sector, you already know the systems, marketing plans, and management techniques that work in the sector you've chosen for your startup. Your business plan would simply capture that knowledge on paper.

3. Lack In Business Management Skills.

A. Along the path to a startup, you will have attached yourself to the best mentor available (usually a manager). You have learned what makes that person tick, how he manages time, how she interacts with employees, what he generally does to make things happen. With this knowledge, you can apply what works, but adapted to your own style.

4. Unaware Of City/Government.

A. Knowing the rules is a must. You might need city licenses, county permits, or other approvals. Before you start your project, check with all officials who could have control over your business to make sure that everything is done in accordance with the regulations. Do your homework.

5. Delay In Collecting Accounts Receivables.

A. The best approach to avoid this problem altogether is to send out invoices in advance. At times I had clients pay retainers. On other occasions, I was able to bill in advance for future work. Another solution is to give your bookkeeper commissions on all receivables collected within a certain timeframe; that financial stake can be a good incentive.

6. Negative Cash Flow.

A. See above. However, at crunch time, stretch out your bill paying as much as you can. Pay the small guy first and delay paying the big guy. Spending on any extras is frivolous until the situation improves; just DON'T do it.

7. **Unpredictable Extraordinary Circumstances**.

A. I don't know the odds of this happening, but I am sure it is low. On the other hand, 9/11 was a tragic extraordinary circumstance that affected a lot of businesses, including mine. When the unpredictable situation is personal, having partners or shareholders can soften the impact on the business because responsibilities can be shared. For example, if you become sick, if you already have the right agreement with one of the partners or shareholders, that person can step in immediately. If you plan for as many contingencies as possible in your company's organizational documents, managing crises will be simplified.

8. **Misconception Of Work Required To Stay In Business.**

A. Your job experience and your prior experience with startups should prepare you for the amount of work needed. You can choose a business where little work on your part is required, as in being a silent partner. You can do this by finding a trustworthy working partner or choosing a business in a non-labor-intensive sector.

9. **May have corruption or unethical behavior.**

A. There's no way to really know this until you get

into a project. If you encounter anyone looking for handouts to expedite your project, for example, stick to the high road and refuse.

10. Dishonest Employees May Be Hired.

A. Again, there's no way to really know about this one either until someone has started working for you. You can get a bead on someone by checking referrals thoroughly. Also, initially limit that person's responsibility and access to company funds and important data until you learn more about him. Still, your company could be a victim of a dishonest employee.

11. Lazy Employees May Be Hired.

A. This rule always worked for me: If you have an employee who doesn't take the initiative within his or her own realm of responsibilities . . . get rid of that employee. You need workers who will go the extra mile and don't have to be told what to do. You should set the example for what you expect.

Formal Business Plan.

The following is what is typically included in a formal business plan. This rather long document reminds me of why I shied away from writing such plans. All or most of these items should be included in a formal business plan.

Part 1

Executive summary
Company objectives
Types of products or services
Target market
Industry or sector
Analysis of competition
Plan for selling your goods or services (marketing plan)
Company advantage over competitors
Any possible marketing plans
Strategies for promoting the business
The price of your goods and services
Distribution for those goods or services
A plan for the web
A description of your marketing team
Organizational structure
Key client list
Legal and insurance

Part 2 Financials

Startup expenses
Projected income
Cash flow statement
Balance sheet
Break-even analysis (how much income is needed to cover expenses)
Capital needed
Budget
Exit strategy

There you have it. Generally, you can use this list to guide you in starting any gig. While I may sometimes think all of this formality isn't necessary, the advantage of compiling. this information is that it allows the iceman to be thoroughly familiar with the details of the business.

8. Fear and Bloating

"In order to succeed, your desire for success should be greater than your fear of failure."
- Bill Cosby

Fear . . . Get over it! I mean, honestly, is striking out on your own a death sentence? No. You are making the leap and creating something. Presumably when you are ready to jump in, you have it well thought out and have minimized the risk. Moreover, if you follow one of the principle points in this book, you have nothing to worry about. That point is to obtain sufficient knowledge in one or more disciplines before you make the leap, so you always have a fallback (get a job!).

Even if you find yourself in over your head with credit and other issues, the end of the world is nowhere on the horizon. You're not going to die! Remember, in business as well as in your personal life, you can always declare bankruptcy and move on with your life. Failure as an American has no stigma. In fact, you will get investors lining up asking you what your next project is.

Fear is creating a mental picture of what might happen to you without evidence that this may occur. Change the illusion and envision sugarplums, or other sweet and more positive stuff. You're no more likely to be doused in sweetness than disaster, but it is a lot more enjoyable to imagine abundance. Fear blocks you from seeing those sugarplums and prevents you from moving forward.

I once had the privilege to attend a three-day Robert Allen seminar. For those of you that don't know, he is one of the pioneers and a leading proponent of buying real estate with no money down. The venue was in Philadelphia, smack in the middle of a cold, nasty winter. I dropped mucho dinero and drove two hours through a snowstorm. The first day of the course, attendees listened to speeches and dealt with schedules and accommodations. The next morning, we dove into the nitty-gritty. As expected, the course detailed ways to structure real estate deals with no money down.
Fine and peachy, except out of nowhere we were suddenly put into groups and told we would be going out that night to raise money for an unspecified charity. Further, we were told in order to pass the course we had to make an acceptable offer to an owner of a property for sale. This was nowhere in the brochure.
Immediately the group's enthusiasm turned into outright fear. The unknown! The unknown! The horror, the horror of it all!

I had horrible visions of braving subzero temperatures to go door to door asking complete strangers for money. I pictured doors slamming, people shouting, and total rejection and dejection crushing me (just like when I asked a girl out on a date). But you know what? None of that stuff happened. We pulled up our bootstraps, tightened our ski jackets so that we looked like clones of the Michelin Man, and hit the streets.

After two hours of begging and collecting, we were instructed to meet the recipients for our fund-raising efforts at a children's hospital. We were shocked to learn our destination was a cancer ward, but the place was lit up like a Democratic convention with bright balloons, posters, and paintings. I saw courageous kids grappling with a death sentence, yet they showed no fear. They greeted us with smiles and gratitude. In return, our hearts went out to them. We humbly presented the $2,000 we had scraped together and left knowing we had just made a difference for those kids. We exorcised our personal fears and learned some valuable lessons.

As instructed, on the final day of the seminar, we tracked down several owners willing to sell their properties with no money down. The whole process was conducted with no anxiety, no hesitation, and no fear. Do you think spending the evening before on a children's cancer ward had anything to do with our change in attitude? It sure did!

Giving us these two assignments was devilishly clever on Mr. Allen's part. He provided a method that removed the wall of fear and the barrier of anxiety, so that we could move on and take action!

Fear: the bane of any true 'iceman.

9. Creativity

*"Success is more a function of consistent common
sense than it is genius."*
- An Wang

Why can't I have strawberry-covered microwave
popcorn? Why can't I use rain as fuel for my car?
These are odd questions, but this is how the creative
mind works. The mind functions in ways quite
different from the way the body functions. However,
the neuron mass nesting inside your beanie needs to be
stimulated, and being inquisitive is one way to
stimulate the neurons to fire. When you ask questions
born in curiosity, you agitate those neurons to come up
with possible solutions. Indeed, if you delve further
into this phenomenon, you will learn that curiosity is
actually at the heart of all scientific methodology.

Curiosity might lead a scientist to form a scientific
hypothesis, a proposed explanation for a phenomenon
that can then be tested. (In logic, a hypothesis means
something different.)

In creating and running a business, the same technique
of stepping out of the box and testing possibilities can
be used. Let me give you a couple of examples from
the businesses I started.
In retail, merchandizing is king. Understanding where
and how to place things is essential. On the surface,

selling items on the street seems cut and dried, but a lot of thought goes into it. Sales were slow one week at my mini-kiosk, so I looked for ways to improve them. I asked myself, what if I move these pink bags to the top shelf. Bingo, sales improved immediately.

In real estate, what if I ask the seller to hold a note? Done! I was able to buy two buildings with none of my own money.

In a franchise, what if we asked company headquarters to reduce our fees and let them use our office as the model for their presentations? Done!

In headhunting, what if we concentrated on supporting only consulting companies? Done! This turned an ordinary agency into a niche with virtually no competition.

In consulting, to offset the high cost of the payroll, what if we paid the consultants we placed when we got paid and gave them an extra 5 percent for their trouble? Done! This allowed us to start this business with much less funding than we would have needed otherwise.

As a final example, what if I slipped a discount coupon for my books into the package of every product I sold on eBay? Done! It improved my book sales significantly.

My mind, as a matter of routine, functions this way.
In the above examples, nothing is original. But the ideas were new to me and appropriate to the business at

hand.

In my book about writing, I said, "It doesn't take a genius to write; it is more like being ingenious." The same applies to creating and developing your own business. Original ideas may come from the minds of geniuses, but there seem to be few true geniuses around today.

Creativity is largely a singular process. However, it may require a team of ingenious folks using their resources wisely to transform one person's idea, one person's eureka moment, into a viable product or service.

One task that cries out for creative thought and serious consideration is naming your business. You can start with the 'what ifs' and go from there. However, deciding on a name is a little more complicated today than just asking yourself questions. The name should signal what your business is all about to everyone who might use the service or buy the product. Because most of you 'icemen' will be using the internet as a marketing platform, in addition to describing what the company does, the name also must contain words that search engine programs will capture. Performing two tasks will help in this process. One is to do a quick search using Google's AdWords' keyword tool to check the hits on words under consideration, while the second is to use a good dictionary. I use this approach for every startup and book title.

A clear example is the title selected for this book. I searched the internet using the keyword tool and discovered that searches for Trump were unusually high. The second resource was the dictionary, where I found that a meaning for 'trump' fit my idea. This is the creative process bolstered by using available resources.

Once your business is up and running, you will continue using available resources.

This leads me to describe a different side of this process: the creative use of resources.

10. Resourcing and Risk

"I've been blessed to find people who are smarter than I am, and they help me to execute the vision I have."
- Russell Simmons, founder of Def Jam

One of the greatest qualities of any iceman is resourcefulness. Using your wherewithal is a significant part of getting any idea off the ground. Most of us don't have the resources of a modern lab, but if we look carefully we can find the means to get our ideas off the ground.

Want to test this? Imagine you saved all your pennies for a deposit on an apartment. Great, but the apartment is empty, minus even a bed to cozy up to the little lady. (Been there, done that). What do you do?

Well, the first thing you do is hit the neighbors up for the free welcome casserole that comes with that lovely microwave dish. You keep the dish until you get the gas running in the oven. Next, you call the hated uncle and the crazy aunt and express the urgent need for furniture. Finally, you hit the street where throwaways suddenly look divine. Surprisingly, you are able to outfit the apartment in a short period of time. Not exactly IKEA, but it represents the essence of being resourceful.

The essential components for resourcing are access to and availability of the things needed to get your project started. Whether those components are people, things, or money, you need to have them at the ready to move forward. In planning your business, most of you will think big. You will have the natural desire to buy the best equipment and supplies to establish the company. I say don't do this. Act as if you have no budget for these items. Minimize your risk when it comes to money. This is one of your most valuable resources and should be used as a last resort.

Take a look around you and see what resources are available and what you have access to before taking the plunge. I have many examples of this. With my main business, instead of buying new phones, I found a company with refurbished phones that sold them with easy credit terms. The entire system was guaranteed for a year.

Finding an out-of-state office for the consulting company was just a matter of converting a small space in the back of the travel agency to function as a satellite office for the consulting company. Integrating the software for recruiting, selling, and billing was ingenious. Using friends to work for free in a bagel store and offering them all the bagels they could eat could be seen as bribery or barter, but either way, they were a tremendous resource.

To sell an inventory of items on eBay, I needed photos. I used my own camera instead of hiring a photographer. As I established my startups, I always looked for ways to do more with less.

By any stretch of the imagination, I am not cheap. Call me sensible and pragmatic. I don't mind taking a risk, but the one resource that business people should guard with their lives is money. We hurt our chances of success when we squander money on unimportant things.

Replace money with your brain: figure out how to get your idea to market effectively without spending all your funds. You have to realize that a lack of adequate funding is the top reason why businesses fail. Use your funding carefully.

Physical resources are all around you for little or no cost. Take advantage of this. Don't blow a huge budget on office desks and chairs, for instance. The money saved on furnishings can be used for more urgent costs such as marketing and paying pesky, unexpected bills.

As far as human resources go, the same practical approach can be used. In establishing relationships with professionals such as accountants, lawyers, and bankers, you want to have good access if at all possible. I was able to accomplish this by using professionals referred by mutual friends and by advising these professionals on their computer systems and marketing, which gave the relationships mutuality.

Quite by accident, I found a lawyer who happened to be a former IRS accountant. He needed help choosing hardware and software for his growing business. I was only too happy to do this for him. I then referred this same fellow to my regular accountants, who began to use him as their lawyer.

This opportunity to provide referrals improved as my main business grew. The consultants who needed both legal and accounting advice were referred to my accountants and my lawyer. As you can expect, these professionals were extremely grateful for the constant flow of business I steered their way.

My regular accountants and my lawyer became friends of mine. Calls to them were always answered immediately or returned within hours.

Bankers are a rather a different breed, yet I also had access to a banker because of mutual friends. Every time I entered the bank, the senior officer greeted me as a friend. In fact, she was always asking if I needed a credit line. I always refused until I actually needed it. Having a resource available when I needed it resulted from building and maintaining strong relationships with key resources.

Another key resource was my trusted secretary.

Not long after renting the space that offered a shared secretary, an increased workload meant that we needed a full-time secretary for our business. She came to us through a classified ad and had little experience, but there was just something about her that made us take the chance. What a score! She was willing to learn, and her motivation was simple. She needed to get out of the house. Her out-of-work husband was driving her nuts.

Initially she was given little responsibility, but I soon realized she had the judgment to make decisions and was willing to go the extra mile. She always took the initiative and eventually became the center all of my operations. I gave her power to run the business in my absence, which allowed me enormous freedom.

I used to take off every Thursday to do whatever I wanted. At times, I would fly off somewhere for an extended weekend. I would return on Monday to find the office still intact. No worries.

On those trips, there was no need to take an electronic device to keep in touch with the office. I don't ever want to be one of those people vacationing at a beach but still tethered to their offices by a smart phone. This is no way to live. There is a better way.

My secretary was my single most valuable resource, and with the assistance of my junior partner, kept the whole office running as smoothly as a Swiss watch.

Whatever business you decide to start, having the right resources with the right people in place will give you flexibility and a stress-free life. Running a small business can do this for you. You are the boss. You are an iceman. Surround yourself with smart business people who can support your personal goals on your terms. Use them to the max when running your small business.

I hope this book will motivate you to start a small business, one that will give you an income and allow you not only to survive, but also to thoroughly enjoy your life. What follows are real-life businesses that I started and ran for several years before eventually moving on to create something new. The small businesses described in this book required little money to start and relied heavily on available resources and assets to get them functioning.

Part Two

11. The Start Ups

"Business opportunities are like buses, there's always another one coming".

- Sir Richard Branson

1. Retail …Something for Everyone.

After graduating from college, I had to find work. The last two years of school prepared me for business by teaching me economics, including concepts such as supply and demand and economic trends. However, what I learned in my first two years of college helped kick-start my iceman ways. After studying merchandizing and buying, starting my business endeavors in retail seemed natural.

Living in any large city presents plenty of opportunities for entrepreneurs. This is especially true in New York City. While shopping on 34th Street one hot summer day, I noticed a few empty stores. This was unexpected given that this street has one of the biggest department stores in the world, called Macy*s. This location is a flagship store for Macy's (bigger and better than the average Macy*s) and should have served as an anchor store for other businesses in the area because it attracts a lot of foot traffic.

Normally stores near a flagship store are fully rented to take advantage of an old expression, "Location, location, location"—meaning your business's location is everything.

Nothing could be truer, yet many of the stores were vacant. By visiting the area several times, I confirmed that the foot traffic was indeed terrific. The next person renting in the area should make a fortune. For the hell of it, I met the landlord for one empty store to ask about the rent. He wanted more than $10,000 a month. That threw me for a loop! However, by asking some key questions during the conversation, I learned that the guy wasn't really interested in renting; he actually wanted to sell the building.

In a moment of clarity and inspiration, I asked about renting the area in front of the store until he sold the property. He looked at me as if I were crazy, but kept the conversation going.

By the time the small talk was finished, we had negotiated a short-term rental for the space directly in front of the building. He was willing to provide a temporary contract outlining my occupancy as a tenant, but he warned that the police still might harass me.

The lease term was limited because he wanted to sell the building. I was able to get an option to rent for additional years as long as he owned the property, but the lease would terminate immediately if the building sold. Other conditions of the lease included a prohibition on the sale of dubious merchandise. This was a "win-win" deal because he now had some income, and I had a storefront.

Now you may be envisioning some sort of fancy kiosk or storefront with an awning of some type, but it wasn't. I just set up a folding table with storage space below. In New York, at the time, there were many street merchants selling goods in front of stores and on every street corner. These characters displayed goods on a blanket that they could quickly fold if the cops came. There were so many complaints about street merchants that finally the city government cracked down. At one point, the merchants were required to get a permit from city hall.

Although I had the protection of the agreement from the landlord, my set-up still looked illicit. Imagine an oversized rickety metal table displaying goods in front of an abandoned building. I thought for sure I would be a targeted by the police.

In reality the police never bothered me. Occasionally, they would come by, see the goods, and even buy a few items. When they did, I had my semi-legal rental agreement at the ready and turned on the charm.

They could have fined me for letting my merchandise take up more than three feet of the sidewalk, which was against the law. At times, I was well beyond this invisible line from the building's front. In hindsight, this took brass balls. However, when you are young and hungry, you don't look at it this way. You are doing something that comes naturally to you: you're becoming an iceman.

With a lease in hand, I now had to decide what to sell and figure out where to buy it.

It was hot, and I noticed many women carrying bags and sweating. I thought of paper fans, a cheap, colorful product that would help relieve the heat for women (now my target market). The next day I borrowed $50 from my roommate and scooted around the city looking for fans.

I ended up in a wholesale district that sold various products including cheap Chinese paper fans. I put on my best face and, acting as if I had been doing this for years, I marched in and announced I wanted to buy products. The clerks asked, "What do you want and how much?" I was embarrassed, because the initial order was small, only four dozen fans. Even so, they welcomed me and sold me the products. After I bought a second-hand table, I was ready for business.

I ran back to my storefront, opened that rickety table, and quickly displayed my new merchandize. It was the grand opening!

Women came by—plenty of them. Intrigued by the idea of staying cool with a fan, many made a purchase. That first day, I sold out within three hours. This went on throughout the summer until the weather cooled and I suddenly realized I had to diversify. In retail jargon, I had to create a 'product mix' (thank that college education). I went back to the same wholesalers and started buying women's bags. I lowered the price of the fans and used them as a 'loss leader' to sell bags. Wow, what a success story.

The beauty of this business was that the mark-up on the fans was 150%. This is atypical. Usually it's about 100% depending on your product line. Because the profits were strong, the business was virtually self-funded. Except for the small initial loan, no up-front money was required to invest in stock or to pay the overhead. From day one, the business was paying for itself. I hung around for two years, learned a great deal, and got quite a reputation for selling useful women's accessories.

The above scenario can be used in any commercial area with a great deal of traffic, wherever an agreement can be reached with a decision maker about the space involved. I am aware of several businesses functioning this way. An Israeli company has negotiated space rights from U.S. and European mall directors to allow the company to conduct business in certain spots within malls. They have no kiosk and sell natural seaweed cosmetics in front of other stores to people coming and going.

Another excellent idea is to use the same technique, but with airports as your base. A friend of mine worked for a business that sold perfumes as a gift item at the boarding end of the airport. The set-up was a little more elaborate, requiring a small kiosk, but it was brilliant. The company made a fortune catering to people who had forgotten to buy a gift for friends back home. This is a built-in audience if there ever was one. The overhead was low and the margins were off the charts.

On a recent trip to Madrid, I noticed new kiosks selling various items in the Madrid metro. I am sure it was just a matter of an entrepreneur finding the right person in the local government and making it happen. Foot traffic and a rentable space = opportunity for icemen.

Funding: The deposit for the lease came from my savings. The funding for the initial merchandise ($50) was borrowed from my housemate. As the business grew, profits were plowed back into buying more merchandize.

Management: This is as close as you get to micromanagement. You are the buyer, you are the seller, and you are the store! You must manage your time, stay on top of the inventory, and know the best time to go to the wholesale markets. Eventually, I hired a kid to assist in selling so that I could buy on the fly.
Marketing: No need for much marketing here. The foot traffic was terrific. At times, I would post a large sign saying "Everything must go . . . Going out of business." Some major retailers throughout New York used this same tactic. Stores were always going 'out of business.' You could walk by four years later, and the sign and the business would still be there. It was effective for me, but finally I realized I didn't need it.

2. **Real Estate…Trumped Adventures**

One of the oldest ways to wealth in America is to own real estate. You can choose to speculate or build a satisfying portfolio through long-term investing. Donald Trump's wealth resulted from both techniques.

Starting out, he did a fair amount of speculating. One of his first projects was an apartment complex in the Midwest. His father bought the complex and invited Donald to manage it. Trump filled the under-used complex with tenants and soon after sold the property for a large profit. The rest is more or less history. Along the journey, 'the Donald' moved more and more away from speculative ventures to ones that spin off income, such as his casinos. No matter how you look at it, real estate is at the core of wealth for Trump and many other Americans.

Real estate is a hard asset: a commercial building, an apartment, or a house. It is tangible and can be bought, sold, or rented if the owner so desires.

My experience with real estate and its true value began, ironically, because of my status a tenant. I was living on Manhattan's Westside in a five-story walk-up containing 'railroad apartments.' These units resemble railroad cars. A hallway runs the length of the apartment. I shared an apartment on the bottom floor with a friend. It took us six months to get the place in livable condition. When we moved in, the place had dilapidated linoleum floors, walls of broken plaster, no electrical outlets, and a bathtub smack in the middle of the kitchen. Still, we saw the potential. After the renovations, friends would come and marvel at the results. It served as a model apartment because some of them moved into the vacant apartments upstairs.

All was good. We now had a reasonably habitable apartment with friends throughout the building. Well, that didn't last long. The landlord sold the property to a New York City cop who had a reputation for shadiness. (We later found out that this guy was on The Village Voice worst landlord list every year). His goal was to empty the rent-controlled building, reconfigure the apartments into studios, and squeeze more rent from future tenants. We would have none of it. We pooled our money, hired a lawyer, and stopped paying the rent.

This really hurt the guy. The apartment next to us magically caught on fire. We set up an all-night crew to watch for further trouble and continued the rent strike until we had a court date. Leading up to the court date, the landlord managed to get one tenant to accept money to move out. He tried this with the rest of us, but we refused his offer.

On the court date, the landlord brought his checkbook and instructed his lawyer to negotiate a settlement. In the end, each of us was given $10,000 to leave. This was significant money at the time. After getting over my emotional attachment to the apartment, I quickly found a place in a semi-legal, commercial building on the East Side.

Remarkably, it happened again. I had a two-year lease, and just when it was time to renew it, the building was sold. The new owner wanted me out so that he could convert the building into condominiums. What to do? It was time to hire a new lawyer and hold out. I did, and in the end I was paid $8,000 to move. This is lightning striking the same person twice. It proved to me the intrinsic value of real estate, although being the landlord in either case would have been horrible.

That was in 1985, when people quickly became millionaires by buying and selling property. My future wife suggested I move to the suburbs. I didn't want to, but the real estate market had me intrigued. The possibilities of buying a house or investing some of my savings in the residential real estate market were enticing. At the time, it was all the rage. The demand was so heated; properties were being bought one day and sold the next for quick profits. The banks and other lenders had fewer regulations.

Wait, doesn't this all sound familiar? It should. It is almost exactly what caused the crisis in 2008. The same conditions existed. The banks would lend money to anyone standing and capable of steaming a mirror.

As an entrepreneur looking to buy his first home, I agreed to look outside of New York. The first thing I did was to explore the building complex where my girlfriend lived. The individual apartments were called co-ops—a type of property ownership. It is a different form of ownership than a condominium or house.

Basically a co-op is a corporation set up to manage the property and issues shares to the owners for individual units. The corporation maintains the common areas such as the outside walls, the roof, and public areas.

If you were a tenant before the building was converted to a co-op, you had the opportunity to purchase your apartment at an inside price—a discount. This allowed for instant equity. My girlfriend—soon to be my wife—bought a few units at the inside price. At that time, a tenant could buy multiple units or strike a deal with a neighbor. We rented the units to tenants and eventually listed them for sale.

A partner and I decided to take advantage of the popularity of apartment building conversions. Because this partner was a real estate agent, he had access to multiple-listing services for properties and to prospective tenants. This is another example of using resources; my partner knew which buildings were headed for conversion. We would rent multiple apartments in one apartment building and then sublet them while we waited for the notice of conversion we knew was coming. Our game plan was only semi-legal, but everyone knew the deal.

Once we received the notice–a preliminary prospectus called, oddly enough, a 'red herring' because of the red print on the cover; we signed agreements to buy the rental apartments and paid deposits for each unit. An important clause in those contracts allowed us to transfer them with no restrictions; we were able to immediately list our own properties for sale. For some of the apartments, we were able to "flip the contracts" for ten times our deposit without the need for bank financing. While the remaining apartments brought a smaller profit, none required a mortgage or note from the bank because they sold so quickly.

What a windfall! We wound up buying or controlling several apartments that sold quickly for tidy profits that allowed me to become a homeowner.

Buying my first home was entirely different compared to the transactions above. This purchase was for personal use. A sales contract was drawn up with signature lines for buyer and seller. The contract was scrutinized by a lawyer and sent to the bank to secure financing. The bank required a deposit with credit check and employment verification. An appraisal, a house inspection, a land survey, and title inspection also were needed. Eventually the bank loan came through. At the closing, we were issued a deed with a mortgage and a lien that the bank held as security. All documents were signed and witnessed by a notary. Taxes for the property were held in escrow and paid in monthly installments. I had married by then, and my wife and I joined the millions of Americans seeing real estate as part of the dream.

Having tasted the promise of real estate as an investment vehicle, I continued the search for more properties. I found two. One was a building with rentable apartments. The owner agreed to hold a note for 20 percent of the purchase price. A bank agreed to finance the remaining 80 percent, treating the owner's note as a deposit. A few months later I was issued a mortgage and had a fully occupied investment property. The mortgage from the bank was in the first position. If I defaulted, the bank would get paid first upon the sale of the building. The seller's note would be paid only after the bank received its money.

The next property I found was a unit in an apartment complex that was being converted to condominiums. I bought this at the same time because the chances of being rejected were nil and slim. I used a different bank to finance this purchase. Banks, credit agencies, and others involved in financing real estate did little cross-checking.

This investment property was nicely landscaped and had broad street appeal. I met the owner who showed me the property, which was fully renovated and in move-in condition. I was about to sign the contract when it occurred to me that not much parking was available on the street, but there appeared to be private garages in the back of the complex. I asked for a garage. The owner initially balked at this because he was selling them separately. I insisted on this, and after some tough negotiating he included it in the contract. The mortgage was approved.

I rented the property to a corporate executive with a guaranteed one-year lease from the company. Six months in, I was informed that the tenant had been transferred. The company paid me the full rent for the remaining six months. I thought I might test the waters for selling it before trying to rent it again.

I listed it for a ridiculously high price. To my surprise, the phone was ringing like crazy. I had buyers bidding against each other. The price, it turns out, was far from being ridiculous. The reason was the garage. The buyers saw it as an incredible benefit in an area where parking was at a premium. The premium for me was a whopping profit. Three months later I walked into my bank with a six-figure check in hand. The surprised bank teller asked me, "Did you win the daily lotto?" I said, "No, real estate bingo."

As mentioned, regulations were pretty loose back then. Enormous speculation and rapid appreciation of properties were widespread. Everyone seemed to be making money. Even with this, I resisted selling the rental property. I was advised by my accountant to use it as a tax shelter. I sold it years later when it was fully depreciated and no longer helped reduce my taxes. When I sold, I took a five-year note. (There's that passive income thing again!)

Indeed the market was hot as a pistol. However, shortly after I sold the condo, everything changed. The interest rates charged by banks hit the roof. Suddenly, those normally qualified for a mortgage were unable to get a loan. You now had to pledge your first-born son! Those with existing notes without an interest cap were severely hurt. Many people went into default or had to declare bankruptcy.

Thank goodness I wasn't one of them. In retrospect, it was an exciting time. Most people who bought homes or investment properties during this period made out like bandits.

Funding: Money for the initial investments came from my settlements for vacating the two apartments in New York. Several of the purchases required no money down. By convincing a property owner to hold a note, I avoided having to pay money out of my pocket, because the bank treated the note as if it were a down payment. This is a strategy I used several times; it's a funding solution that should be explored by everyone in this game.

With other deals, we signed a sales contract but turned the property over so quickly that we didn't have to secure a mortgage. We did this by asking for a long time period before closing to secure financing and by including a clause in the sales contract that let us transfer the contract without securing financing. In a hot real estate market, this strategy for controlling real estate works really well.

We did have to pay 'consideration' or earnest money at the time we signed the contracts. I funded these good-faith deposits from profits on previous transactions.

Management: Management was pretty easy except when I went beyond individual units. With the apartment building, I decided to use staggered leases with different dates for renewals to make it more likely that the building would never be vacant. There was always some income. In addition, all the leases were strong, legally favoring the landlord as much as possible. With single units, the laws generally favor the landlord, while the laws in most states are different for multiple dwellings. Rent control or rent stabilization rules may exist. It is much easier to vacate or evict a tenant for non-payment in a single unit. Collecting rent became a breeze, especially when I got my charming, strapping cousin to show up to collect it.

Marketing: You need a business card that lists you as a Real Estate Buyer and Seller. (Generally no license needed). Using classified ads for buying and selling is a must. Listing a property with a competent real estate agent is well worth the commission. Running ads for apartments two months in advance when possible is a particularly smart thing to do. Joining forces with a Realtor as a resource is the best thing to do!

3. Travel Agency; High Flying Franchise

Soon my wife became anxious about the financial burden we just took on in buying a house and other property. She didn't want to work for someone else any more than I did. The solution was to find a business.

Her background included working as a tour guide and booking agent for small companies, making a travel agency a logical business for us to buy. This business provides airline tickets and package tours for clients.

This was a logical choice because of her experience. For me, the allure of travel made the business enticing.

As an iceman, I am always looking for opportunities and the thrill of creating something new. As a result, I read the classified ads religiously. Most newspapers have a section on businesses for sale. The Sunday editions of daily newspapers have the most and the best of these ads.

One Sunday morning, armed with my morning cup of java and the Sunday paper, I turned to the classified section and began the search. When I checked the 'businesses for sale' section, what do I see—Travel Agency for sale. Fantastic! I made the call and to my surprise learned that the business was just down the road from our new house. I made arrangements to meet the owner/seller.

After the obligatory small talk at our first meeting, I asked a key question: "Why are you selling?" This is a fundamental question that should always be asked. When you buy a business, you are buying the good, the bad, and the ugly. Keep this in mind. As the potential new owner, you want to hear about this and later try to minimize the bad and the ugly. You don't want their overwhelming headaches. By asking why the owner is selling, you want to find out something about the bad and the ugly. It is also an excellent way to determine how motivated the seller is.

This seller had an understandable reason for selling. Because she had developed health problems, the traveling required for the business had become too much for her. My wife and I now knew the seller was motivated, but we had to dig deeper to identify some of the day-to-day problems she encountered. Was the health problem related to work, was there a problem with the landlord, was there enough business to sustain the business and go forward? Ask your questions in a polite, friendly, business-like manner. If you are unsatisfied with the answers, dig deeper—ask more questions.

The next step is to do a little observation. An obvious thing to take note of was whether clients were coming in. We purposely set up the meeting at lunch hour when most people would take some time to shop for travel. Indeed, a few clients walked in to inquire about trips and vacations. We also noticed how unorganized she was. Files and paper work were all over the place with no client software.

My wife's many talents include her organizational skills. This was in our favor. We figured that by organizing and computerizing client records, we could improve business by 20 percent.

While making our observations, we kept asking questions: How long have you been established? Why did you get into the business? What do you like and dislike about the business? These types of questions lead to more, so listen carefully. By the time you are finished with your 'polite inquisition,' you should be able to determine whether you want to move forward with negotiations.

We did, and the negotiations proceeded. We had learned that the business was a franchise. Picture a franchise as being a huge wheel. In the center is headquarters where marketing, branding, and other programs are developed for the units at the end of the spokes. It's a system to deliver goods or services in a consistent manner using headquarters' good name or brand. This brand, sometimes called a trade name or trademark, is licensed to the units or franchisees.

Good franchises are easily identifiable. When your business is part of a franchise, you don't have to start from scratch on branding and can take advantage of the franchisor's ability to develop programs, purchase goods or services in bulk, and continually promote the business. Of course, in the grand old U.S.A., franchises such as McDonald's, Burger King, and Dunkin' Donuts are well known. (Notice they are all food).

But there is a price. The franchisee (agency) must pay fees. These ongoing fees may include franchise fees, royalty fees, advertising fees, and service fees, on top of the initial fee to become part of the franchise. Once a franchisee is operational, it is granted exclusive territorial rights. Some franchisors offers financing; others don't. There are strict rules and policies for how the business should operate.

Intrigued, as a prospective franchisee, I requested a meeting with the people in headquarters—more due diligence. I ascertained the requirements for financing, the fees, and the territories available, and got a general feel for how the franchisor promoted the business.

Satisfied, I went back to the owner and negotiated a price with financing. The price was much less than the initial investment required by the franchisor. Moreover,

I was able to get the owner to take a personal note with a small deposit. The deposit came from friends of ours who were interested in the travel discounts they could receive as co-owners of a travel agency. We obtained a new five-year lease with better terms from the building landlord. With no money of our own and within four weeks, this turnkey business was under new management. Ours!

My wife immediately took to the business, a natural for her. She made some procedural and organizational changes, implemented a marketing plan, created a client supplier list, and installed new software for tracking sales and customers. In addition, she hired an agent experienced in booking business clients. The company took off. Within six months, the business improved beyond our initial estimates by 40%.

This business was a perfect match for an iceman. The main advantage of owning a travel agency, of course, is the travel benefits. And boy, did we ever take advantage of it. The suitcases were always packed, and at a moment's notice we were off to some exotic location. What is the point in having your freedom if you can't travel?

Funding: The funding for this venture came out of the pocket of the seller. She was motivated to find a qualified buyer and would have done almost anything to sell. She accepted a personal promissory note as payment for the business. It was risky, and I recommend never signing a personal note if it can be avoided. We negotiated a low interest rate for the loan, and it cost us almost nothing to get into this business.

Management: With my wife's organizational skills, managing this business was easy. Moreover, the person we hired to develop the business accounts had some management experience. The franchisor trained the rest of the staff to act as independent agents. The training allowed for individual decision making and gave the agents the ability to function as a manager on any given day.

Marketing: As a franchise, the agency could rely on headquarters for most of the marketing and advertising. With the new software in place, we were able to follow up on all inquiries and convert most of them to sales. Follow up is the key to this business.

4. **Headhunting : Searching For Talent.**

You should know by now that my main business was "headhunting." Headhunting is a term used for agencies that identify and approach qualified candidates who seek employment in any number of business sectors. In most cases, the company (client of the agency) pays a finder's fee or placement fee when the person is hired. Fees are based on the starting salary of the employee. Sometimes a company will give an agency a retainer (advance payment) in order to facilitate the hunt.

This is the business that I had for many years, and it served as a springboard to many others. I had begun learning this primary discipline in my fourth full-time stint as an employee. I gained many skills from my other jobs, but working for the headhunting company gave me a taste of what it was like to function in a professional environment and increased my desire to have my own professional business. The organizational and marketing systems used at this company served as a template for my own headhunting agency and later startups.

As I stated earlier in this book, the path I chose was to put the experiences learned from these early jobs into starting my own businesses.

Tactically, this is less risky than starting something for which you have no background. I venture to say a lot of startups are a result of partners, employees, and others in an organization concluding they could do better on their own. If you find yourself in this position, before you leave, learn as much as you can and remember to do your homework to make sure you will be in a growth industry.

With that said, what follows are some of the details, thoughts, and resources used to set up this business up.

After doing research, I had determined there was plenty of room for more headhunting services in the software sector. The starting salaries were trending upward, and the demand for skilled technicians continued to grow.

Workers in this field earned good money with only three years of experience. This makes a significant difference in your expected income and fees.

Here is an example. At the time, with two years of experience in the software field, an employee's average salary was $40,000. The same years of experience in the hospitality sector (hotel and restaurant employees) would be about $25,000. Check out the difference for a fee agreement with a 20 percent rate. In the case of the software employee, the fee would be $8,000 dollars. In the hospitality example, it would be only $5,000. This difference makes an enormous impact on your bottom line.

With the decision to go forward out of the way, a final crucial decision remained: choosing a partner.

Finding a good partner is invaluable when you start out. The right person relieves you of the enormous pressure some entrepreneurs feel when going it alone.

Later, it will allow you a considerable amount of freedom. Finding the right person is easier than you might think. The first thing to do is find someone in the same line of business. Ask your clients for the names of people who are enjoyable to be around, who have excellent communication skills, and who have been successful for them. This is an old headhunter's secret. Once you get some names, call each potential new partner and say that a mutual client recommended him/her.

During the screening and recruiting process, you will find some surprises. The biggest surprise is that most of the recommendations will be people who are already business owners, not employees.

You can approach these people with the idea of joining forces or buying them out. If you have the resources, buying or buying a share of an existing business can be a good approach, with obvious advantages. However, the real concern for any iceman—for you and the person you are approaching—is who controls the business.

Most established small business owners are closely attached to the entity and quite reluctant to give up control. If you find a potential buy-in, first discuss who will have the controlling interest. Otherwise, you will be wasting your time. The better option is to buy the business outright.

The other prospects recommended by your clients should be qualified as well. They may be employees at their companies, but when a client recommends them, they are flattered and become 'all ears' when you say are seeking a partner. As a professional recruiter, you are trained and skilled at determining who is right for the job. But this is not just a job. You are seeking a partner. You will need to go a little deeper and find out more about each candidate's needs and motivations.

Another option is to go after a potential partner directly, using those professional recruiter skills. Instead of asking a client to recommend someone, recruit someone directly from your competition.

If I had a nickel for every time I heard employees from

a competitor say they wish they were in their own business, I could have retired a long time ago . . . well, maybe not, but I would have had a head start on retirement! When considering entrepreneur wannabes, the first question should be "Why haven't they started their own business?"

Maybe the answer is that they just need a motivational nudge or they lack the wherewithal. You may be the solution to those obstacles. You can approach them to see if this is the case.

Make sure they are on the same page and they will bring skills or other attributes unavailable in your own repertoire. They also may be able to contribute new clients and inside knowledge of systems and management. Before you make an offer, make sure you check that person's references. Ask clients of your potential partner what they think about this individual's production and service.

Offer your potential new partner an interest in the new company through stock options, stock distribution, or a simple agreement for sharing a certain amount of the profits. Once you have selected a working partner, you are your way.

Another key resource or talent you will need is a competent accountant, as mentioned in the section on passive income. You will need an accountant's help to form the business and will rely on them for ongoing advice. In choosing an accountant, you may want to get references from your network of friends and business associates. This works well because most of those people in your sphere will know your intentions and motives. But don't stop. You must interview at least three before making a choice. This is a crucial resource; you need to find someone who is current with accounting procedures and has experience with startups. Your accountant should be able to present options and explain things in layman's terms and should be accessible and professional. Finally, look for someone you would be comfortable socializing with at a cocktail party!

In the end, I actually got lucky in my accountant choice, after several interviews, including one disaster held in an office directly adjacent to the subway, where we mostly sat and yelled at each other because of the continuous rumble of the trains. How could anyone function in this setting? How did they hear the phone ring? It's always amazed me to see professionals carry on like this as if nothing is askew.

My luck involved finding a startup accounting firm that was hungry for new business. These accountants were aggressive without ever overstepping the laws or procedures. Our businesses grew side by side and allowed us to experience similar problems and solutions to those problems.

Other important issues come down to the physicality of being in business. Where are you going to locate? Not near a subway! You'll need telephone lines, computer systems, and other necessities. Does a home office come to mind? It should. When starting out, look to this as a temporary solution that will cut down on initial expenses.

My partner and I created my main startup by putting an extra phone line in my new partner's house and installing software on her home computer. I was still employed at that point, selling IT services to clients of a consulting firm (see "Selling Advice"), but I was able to help my partner using contacts I had. Meetings with clients were set up at neutral locations such as restaurants. This worked wonderfully well until the business grew so fast we needed extra help and a real office for conducting further business.

With some money in the pocket in the form of a retainer and cash flow rising, it was time to locate some space. Again, use your resources.

One phone call to my accountant pointed me to a shared office facility close to that accounting firm. This was a full suite of small businesses sharing one secretary supplied by the landlord. In addition, the suite was outfitted with phone and computer lines and essentially ready to move in. With the recommendation of my accountant, the landlord was willing to accept one month's rent as security and gave us two months' free rent.

What remained was a paint job. This time the use of a personal resource came into play. An indebted cousin was more than happy to paint, clean, and do whatever was necessary to get back on my good side. A done deal! In one week we were up and running. We were now a professional firm with three employees: My partner and I and a shared secretary. By then, I had left the security of employment for the freedom and potential of being the majority owner of a new company.

This was one dynamic company and one with unlimited growth. The more software companies such as Microsoft introduced new products, the more clients needed to find employees with new skills. The growth eventually led us to build a team of ten people and hire a competent full-time secretary, which allowed me to do what I wanted to do: play and start other businesses.

Funding: A retainer of ($5,000) from a client proved to be a real key in this set-up. It also helped that initially I was still receiving a steady paycheck from my employer. The retainer was used to set up my new partner's home office and later to help pay the expenses for the other office. In reality, very little out-of-pocket money was used to create this venture. I waited to quit my job until my income from the business was enough to replace my paycheck. I was now able to really focus my energy on making money for my partner, my employees, and myself.

Management: One of the traits I looked for in my partner was the ability to manage. I got that and a whole lot more. When we began expanding, we developed a procedural and training manual to ensure new employees stayed on message. In addition, I personally trained all new employees in the use of in-house recruiting software for a two-week period. The entire staff was given a set of monthly goals and rewarded with extra commissions when they exceeded them. The tone was set from the top. It was a relaxed, open environment where all were allowed to seek help, share, and function to the best of their ability. Finally, my secretary, who stayed with us for more than 10 years, proved to be an incredibly invaluable resource.

Marketing: In recruiting a partner from my direct competition, I wound up doubling the client base. We now had more clients than we could handle. As an aside, if you find yourself in the same situation, apply the 80/20 rule. Spend your time and resources on the 20 percent of your clients giving you 80 percent of the business. You won't know this until you are in business for a while, but do the review shortly after (18 months) and you will be rewarded tenfold. Use the normal promotional tools—business cards, a website— but go several steps further and have lunches with your better clients, host Christmas parties, and send personalized thank-you notes.

5. Hi Tech Consulting Advice

Software consulting or IT consulting was a spin-off of the technical recruiting firm. The idea was to get direct contracts from the clients for temporary assignments. This was fairly easy to do. We had the client base and just needed to inform them that we now offered this service. We did this by hiring an experienced salesman and a recruiter who had other clients. The recruiter was an older woman who looked and acted like Mae West. She had a memory like an elephant. She could read a resume once and remember the minute details months later. Her desktop was bare because she had no need to keep anything there. She would spit out endless quips that kept clients laughing beyond control. Her husband (a consultant) was rich. I once asked why she needed to work. She said, "For 20 years, I stuffed envelopes, stuffed turkeys, and stuffed his face. It's time to get my own stuff."

Consulting is different from full-time placement. Essentially, the plan called for us to find qualified technicians and rent them to the corporations. You can see the similarities. The same amount of work went into finding the talent. However, the financial rewards were greater.

As a consulting firm, we were now responsible and accountable for both small and large projects for our clients. We set this business up as a subsidiary to the main corporation. We used the same office, support staff, and methods to get the job done. The biggest difference between the consulting business and the recruiting business was that the consulting business required a much larger amount of capital. The business at a basic level was a payroll company, once the consultant has been supplied. Let me explain.

A client releases a job requirement for a project that is budgeted for six months. The client describes the consulting position and task with earmarks and milestones to be met by the temporary worker. We are tasked with finding someone who meets those requirements. We scrub our database and indeed find a suitable person.

Knowing the budget or daily rate lets us negotiate with the consultant. The client has offered us a rate of $600 a day for a seven-hour day. That is more than $85 per hour. We offer the independent consultant $50 per hour, and everyone is happy. The project lasts the entire six months with our firm grossing about $72,000. The independent contractor, who was responsible for paying his own taxes and benefit costs, grosses about $42,000 for working half a year. This hiring method was perfect for corporations because they didn't need to pay for benefits such as health insurance nor make a long-term commitment.

From the example above, you can see the potential for making enormous profits. As enticing as this looks, you need to make a thorough analysis and projections before you start this business.

The trick with this business is having adequate financing. Imagine if suddenly you had 10 people on billing—in other words, you had to pay the salaries of ten people. These costs could be a deal breaker. The consultants had to get paid. Some of our clients agreed to pay us within 30 days, but others wouldn't agree to that. We offered contractors working for slower-paying clients the option of getting an extra five percent in pay if they were willing to wait a bit for payday. Still, making payroll was difficult.

A basic spreadsheet will show what monies are needed to support the number of people on billing. For a while, we were able to support the initial number of consultants on billing by shifting monies from the recruiting firm, borrowing from my Shove It Fund, and even borrowing from friends. All of this was a temporary Band-Aid. But it worked! It gave us enough breathing room until other financing could be put in place.

However, this money crunch caused me a lot of stress.

I found myself going to the gym a lot more. If I had to do it again, I would have had the money in place before jumping in. But we icemen always see the upside and are willing to deal with the stress and pressure that can accompany you on the path to independence. I think there can be a correlation between stress and being responsible for generating large sums of money. Don't look at all those zeros and feel intimidated. Treat the numbers as if you were just doing basic math.

Keep your focus on satisfying the clients and doing what you do best. Create, implement, and manage your resources to get the job done.

Eventually, the cash flow situation worked itself out and funding the payroll (see below) was no longer needed. We were happy to see that day. We were even happier that we got into the business.

Funding: Our finance solution was the use of an outside payroll funding company. These types of companies manage your receivables and outlay the funds needed for your payroll. They get their money back when you receive your money from the client. They earn profits with service fees and commissions.

Management: Because most of the tasks for this business are similar to recruiting tasks, we just needed to add new software to manage the hours and billing for consultants working for our clients. This firm's sister company, the headhunting business, did the recruiting, using systems already in place.

That process—finding qualified candidates—turned out to be the hardest part of this business. We would receive orders for consultants and would quickly disseminate them to the recruiters. After we tweaked the system to handle consultancy better, we cut response times in half. Responding quickly was a priority as the business was dynamic with a lot of competition. I continued to do the training while allowing the new recruiter ('Mae) to manage the recruiting team.

Marketing: Hiring an experienced salesman was a smart move. He brought several accounts over with him, so we had a good start. This business required a lot of schmoozing and handholding with clients. All of the recruiters were taught to ask the consultants where their last contract was as part of obtaining references, and this information was then used as to develop leads for our sales team. An independent website and a newsletter highlighting our successes along with the various changes in the industry had our marketing efforts motoring along.

6. Bagel Store; Real Dough!

A bagel store is a bread maker—both metaphorically and literally. Literally it is a plant that produces a kind of bread made famous in the Jewish community. Flour is formed in a circular fashion and baked to give it a thin crust. In the New York area it is extremely popular and copied throughout the United States. The flour is called dough. The metaphor: Dough is slang for money or cash.

In the commerce sector, you can classify this type of business as food production, light manufacturing, or retail. Our set-up was all three. We prepared, baked, and sold food products at the retail level.

My involvement in this business was a fluke. On a day off, I was enjoying a slice of pizza in a strip mall.

Within the mall is a supermarket where I bought my groceries. This supermarket was an anchor store for the mall. As I was leaving the supermarket, I saw a 'for lease' sign on a storefront directly next to the supermarket exit. It was the original location of the pizza store where I had just eaten. The wheels started to turn, producing ideas about what type of store would be good in this location.

I called an acquaintance of mine living in the neighborhood. We met at the pizza shop's new location for a slice. While there we had a conversation with the guys behind the counter. One of the guys said, "If I had the money, I would start a bagel shop." I turned to my friend and without speaking knew immediately what had to be done: Meet the landlord. We quickly got the name of this person and set up a meeting.

Our first meeting was polite and informal. She (the landlord) requested a business plan. Although she liked the idea, she was reluctant to rent the space to two guys never before in the bagel business.

The problem was solved when I produced a business plan including a strategy, traffic numbers, and growth charts highlighting the potential for the store. At this same meeting, she proposed a five-year lease with rental numbers that were off the chart. She also wouldn't offer a free rental period during the build-out and demanded a personal guarantee. We left the meeting feeling disappointed, but we knew we had conveyed our seriousness about renting the space. We proposed an additional meeting in which we made a counteroffer. With further negotiating, our terms were accepted—we got the key, a 10-year lease with two months' free rent, and increases tied to the Consumer Price Index.

Elated, we put the plan in motion. The first thing needed was an architect's plan and a building permit, both required by the building department. This took three weeks to get. This was a clue as to what was coming. Once the project was approved, we immediately started demolition of the old place and began construction. Luckily, a pizza store and bagel store have things in common. Both produce food and have some of the same equipment for doing so. We used this to our advantage. Even with this head start, we ran into problems.

One of the biggest problems was discovering we needed to provide an accessible bathroom for disabled people. This was a new requirement for all restaurants; wheelchair access was mandated now in all building codes. This, of course, altered the initial building plans. After submitting revised plans, we won approval and moved forward.

We were now six weeks into the project with no actual construction begun. Most of the time was spent in demolishing what had to go and rounding up building supplies. A garbage strike coincided with the demolition. We literally had to haul the demolished material to the town dumps. Then we discovered that the initial plan was based on old equipment specifications. The new equipment wasn't going to fit. We had to go back to the drawing board. This meant finding either old furnishings or custom-made equipment. Through research, we found a supplier who assured us that the equipment could be modified.

As you can see, this project was far from being a straightforward renovation. It was a construction nightmare. In our sixth month, a serious problem arose.

We discovered that the machines and other equipment weren't going to function properly because the floors in the space weren't level. The entire floor had to be ripped up, the support structure leveled, and the flooring replaced. This little project took an extra month.

By this time, we were over budget, and funding for the project was nearly depleted. I should mention those funds came from a second mortgage on our house. My wife thought I was crazy.

So did my partner. In the tenth month of the project, with little money or energy left, he approached me with a buy-out proposal. He wanted to sell his share of the partnership to a third party. That individual proposed a "lowball offer" for my share too—so low, it didn't cover my investment. I decided his terms were that of a vulture hovering over a soon-to-be-dead carcass. Needless to say, I dropped the negotiations with this chap. I went back to my partner and convinced him that we could finish the job.

We needed cash to buy the necessary equipment. We bought it using my credit cards. I tapped money lines and all other available credit. I even borrowed money from my company in New York. The last remaining piece of equipment was a specially modified oven.

We went to the manufacturer to arrange financing. They refused because they had leasing companies they work with. I couldn't apply to these companies because my credit lines were now maxed out. One solution was available—asset financing. I went back to the manufacturer and negotiated (begged) for him to give me the oven with a promissory note. It was unusual for the manufacturer to consider that option. He eventually acquiesced, albeit with tough terms. He demanded a six-month note with high interest and virtually no grace period. The note included a lien on the equipment we just bought—ouch! The worst clause in the agreement gave him the ability to take complete control of the store if a single payment was late or delinquent.

We had no choice. We rolled the dice for perhaps our last time. The special oven was delivered in the eleventh month. Immediately after the oven was installed, I went back to the building department to get a certificate of occupancy. We were now finally in operation, but with no working capital. We borrowed money from friends to obtain the necessary supplies to make the product. The week before we opened, we found a baker and a roller. A roller: hand-rolls the product. Unbeknownst to them, we were broke. The agreement called for them to get paid after one week. The pressure and the excitement were almost too much to handle.

Before opening, I called friends and asked them to work at the store for free. On the day of the grand opening, I had eight friends show up to help. Thank goodness—the line of customers was out the door. We had that new oven cranked to 500 degrees and baking product the whole day. We sold every bagel and all the available products in the store.

What a relief! We were finally open and had working capital. We now were able to buy more supplies and get through the first weekend. At the end of that first weekend, my partner shook my hand, gave me a hug, and thanked me profusely for hanging in there.

The store went on to be an unqualified success, earning free publicity in magazines and newspapers as the best bagel in the area. Within six months, the oven was paid off, and within ten months my total investment was returned. Way to go—way to make dough!

Funding: Financing this project was scary and just about took all my resources. A second mortgage on my house was used for most of the construction and labor. In addition, we went considerably past the two-month 'build out' period, so we had to pay rent for months before we opened and started earning money. I tapped several credit card lines and also used money from my 'Shove It Fund.' As mentioned, we had arranged for all employees to be paid a week after we opened. The week's receipts were enough to pay them and buy all needed supplies to move forward.

Management: This is a cash business, so you totally need someone you trust at the till. My partner and I each had one trustworthy person present at all times to address this. We had to keep track of inventory always and reorder supplies as needed, although this could be handled by one of the employees. We did hands-on training for all procedures and customer relations.

Marketing: The location was outstanding. Being next to an anchor store—in this case a supermarket–saved us a lot of money on advertising. Occasionally, we would use direct-mail coupons designed by an advertising firm, to flood the local market. The coupons always had an offer. "Buy a dozen bagels . . .

and get two free." Another marketing strategy was to diversify the items in the salad bar. This business was an amazing success story!

7. E-commerce, El Bodega Grande

While running the consulting company, I began to use the internet and learned about E-commerce, also known as E-business. A big part of the internet is the use of Electronic Data Interchange or EDI. This exchange of information between businesses over the internet allows for the flow of emails, software, databases, and internet tools. EDI also is used to collect data, reach prospects, and manage clients. As a result of this, the technology businesses became more efficient and effective.

The second part of the E-commerce world is using it to buy and sell goods over the net. Known as online retail and sometimes called e-tailing, this virtual method for selling was contrary to well-known retailing methods up to that point—the idea seemed farfetched for three main reasons. The first is people like to see and feel what they are buying, the second is that they desire 'instant gratification'—being able to use the product right away, and the last issue was security—people wanted to know their financial information was protected.

To improve security, the internet community created new encryption methods and security techniques. As this was being standardized, more brick-and-mortar retailers came into the fold.

Companies both large and small recognized the potential of the net as a distribution channel. Large retailers like Macy*s, Sears, and others set up websites that were virtual catalogs. Small companies took photos of their inventory and followed suit. This visual display along with good descriptions satisfied some of the 'touch and feel' resistance of the public. The issue with instant gratification is ongoing; however, improvements with shipping and well-organized inventory systems shortened the delay.

The public's fear of buying things on-line slowly dissolved as people discovered the benefits. This was evident when Amazon, launched in 1996, announced a $1 billion quarter in 2002. Online retailing was no longer an idea; as busy people began to rely on the internet to save time, it became reality.

In 2008, online sales generated over $200 billion in sales. With the market growing by 17 percent a year and with only 10 percent of the world wired, the potential is enormous.

My first personal experience with E-commerce, in what some may designate a third leg of the internet, focused on auctions. Auctions are part of e-tailing. This platform for selling and distribution was developed by eBay. This is a handy method for allowing multiple buyers the opportunity to bid on products. This is highly effective for individual items. In the beginning, I used eBay to auction off the watch collection that I had accrued over many years (see my book series, Treasures in Time). I had decided it might be time to see what the value of my collection was. I set up the account, took photos of the watches, created the listings, and posted the items. The watches sold like hotcakes. It was fun, and along the way I met some amusing people.

While auctions are great to sell a collection or unwanted stuff, there are more reliable ways to make money online.

A better way is establishing a store. Setting up an online store is relatively easy and inexpensive. I effectively set up an online store for free. No money, no scratch . . . nada. Here, is what I did. I was strolling around the city one balmy afternoon and wound up in a wholesale district. I noticed many different people walking in and out of these places with tons of merchandise. Out of curiosity, I casually walked into one of these places and inquired about the merchandise. Sure enough, everything was for sale and all of it at wholesale prices. I asked the owner if he had a catalog. When he said no, I decided on the spur of the moment to offer my services as a photographer to create a catalog.

Brilliant idea! He was receptive to the idea, and after I explained that I lived in the neighborhood and had considerable expertise (some) photographing merchandise, he allowed me to take some merchandise for me to photograph to prove my abilities. Two days later, I returned to show him the results. His face lit up. I told him that I could photograph the rest of the merchandise and give him a disk. At this point, he allowed me to take anything I wanted to complete the rest of the catalog.

Do you see where I am going with this? After creating a disk for his catalog, I uploaded a copy to eBay and started to sell immediately. The only risk was that an item might not be in stock when I received an order. On every visit I made to the warehouse to fill orders, I checked that all the items I was advertising were still available.

Through attrition and experiment, I quickly keyed in on best sellers and was able to stay on top of the inventory. Meanwhile, on eBay, it appeared that I had a complete inventory of merchandise. After a year of doing this, I was able to buy what I wanted without any worries, using the profits from sales. This is a true story. The owner was so thankful for the increase in business that he occasionally threw in free items when I was there.

This is weird but also true. The very first deal I made on eBay went sour. Sometime before I began selling watches (see The Business of Hobbies, below) and reselling items from the wholesaler in my neighborhood, I had purchased several pairs of Moroccan leather slippers and put them up for sale.

Within two days, I sold a pair to a woman executive who was traveling for her company. She gave me a shipping address in Mexico. Now imagine, I am not only excited about the sale, but also I am eagerly awaiting my first ever positive comment. It didn't happen. After two weeks of waiting, I noticed I got a negative comment from my first buyer. What happened? She never got the item.

This was an inauspicious start to what I am hoping was a way to make some extra income with little effort. It turns out leather products were not allowed into Mexico. Whoa . . . who knew? The slippers were sitting in a customs office somewhere in Mexico. With the help of the local post office, I was able to retrieve them. I quickly contacted the woman and explained the situation, and she profusely apologized for the negative comment. She gave me an address of a co- worker who lived elsewhere, but was about to travel to Mexico. She finally got the item. She contacted eBay and had the negative comment changed to positive.

Here is my takeaway from this. First, you can't control everything in the E-commerce world. Secondly, if at all possible, check the shipping and customs policies before you list an item. Thirdly, when selling on any site where a customer can make comments . . . don't freak out if you get negative feedback . . . or no feedback at all.

Initially, you may feel the thrill of selling and the anticipation of receiving positive comments, but this is not the whole game. The actual game is providing honest and trustworthy service while selling quality things that people want or need. Moreover, busy customers are not always going to take the time to leave a comment, whether positive or negative. Just know that how you respond to a negative comment will determine whether an unhappy customer can be changed to a happy one.

I still maintain this store; however, because eBay has increased fees, cutting my profits, I expect to eventually move over to a Commerce site, where I will set up my own web store. These sites have a lower fee structure than eBay, they host your custom website using their templates, and they do not do auctions.

Two to consider are 'Core Commerce' and 'Big Commerce.' A big plus for these sites is that although there is a small subscription fee for a basic level of service, there are no other fees, so the seller isn't forking over a percentage on each sale. The big negative: you will have to spend money on marketing. However, once you get steady traffic, you are on your way.

Selling merchandise is not the only way to earn income on eBay; you can also use its considerable traffic to make money, as a friend of mine did. He ran a company that financed any item from cars to municipal city dump trucks. He approached eBay about using his financing for big-ticket items. After two years of negotiations, eBay allowed him to stick a small ad on its pages when anyone either won an auction or bought a big-ticket item. In other words, finance your new purchase through this company.

Wow, what a success. My friend set this up knowing that he would be unable to finance all the equipment and purchases, but so his ingenious solution was to set up a referral service with banks. The result was that he got to pick the clients with the best credit and give the others over to the various banks as referrals. So what is the big deal? Well, for each client who clicked on his ad and was passed on to a bank, he received from 50 cents to a dollar from the banks. Imagine the traffic at a gigantic site such as eBay, which gets millions of visitors a day; his little ad was getting thousands of clicks each day. The money added up quickly. This is a splendid example of an iceman using his knowledge of finance and negotiating to make a bundle of residual income. He accomplished this with little money.

Just the other day, he dropped me a line to say his contract with eBay had ended, but the clicks keep coming even as he was negotiating for a new contract.
So here is what you need to set up in E-commerce: A website, descriptions, other content, and photos to display your products. (Yes, of course you also need the products or access to the products.) Next, you need to decide where you want to hang your sign—where do you want your virtual storefront? There are many virtual malls and different selling portals; Yahoo, MSN, and Amazon are just three examples.

In the past, you also needed a merchant account. This allowed you to receive credit card payments online. It took time for the payments to be routed and eventually deposited into your bank account. This was a cumbersome and expensive way to do business.

Today a company such as eBay provides the website for your virtual store and handles the payment process through a sister company called PayPal. Merchant accounts are no longer required. Most transactions are conducted without a hitch.

From personal experience, I believe there are two key items that the online store or website must have: excellent photos and detailed descriptions of the items.

In fact, the more information you provide, the higher the sales. Go beyond color, size, and weight. Write or hire someone to write a thorough outline for each product. Include the benefits for each item. This whole process takes a little more time, but I assure you more customers will stay on the page and make the purchase. As an added benefit, you are creating more relevant content, which search engines love.

Running a store on the net is similar to running it as an 'offline retailer.' However, the online store has several advantages; the low startup cost, minimal expenses, and no overhead for a physical store make this attractive. Remember the net is global with 24-hour availability. Your store is always open and can generate money all day. An additional advantage is that, when you are buying your products from another company, you generally don't have to maintain an inventory. The speed of the system allows you to order only the products you need. You can also choose to let the suppliers do fulfillment and drop ship the product directly to your customer, which will save you time and space.

For beginners, the best place to park your store is eBay,

in spite of fees that are higher than they used to be.

After seeing how quickly my watch collection sold on the site, I opened a store on eBay with products obtained from the wholesaler I mentioned earlier. Initially, I struggled with taking the photos, describing the products, and using the right keywords for titles. The watches had been easy to photograph and describe compared to these products.

As with my first storefront business, I learned through trial and error and responded quickly to feedback to resolve problems. This is yet another advantage of the net. If things aren't working, you can easily change them and see the results almost immediately.

As the owner and buyer for my store, I keep my eye out for good deals and a variety of items, but I mostly rely on two or three wholesalers who offer not only a good variety of products but also good terms.

To this day I maintain a store on eBay that effectively runs itself. It continues to amaze me. Every day I get orders from around the world, and the bank statement shows more money to play with.

Funding: A credit card and bank were used to set up the eBay and PayPal account. Registering with both these entities couldn't be easier. Future eBay subscription payments (required if you have an eBay store) and fees are directly deducted from these accounts. This business easily funds itself from profits after several cycles of selling. If you already have a computer and online connection, as I did, you're ready to start. If you decide to go the route of E-commerce using Core Commerce or Big Commerce, take advantage of their offer of one month free. This will allow you time to set the website up correctly. Consider buying products from wholesalers who drop ship. In effect, you become the middleman with no real cost outlays. E-commerce remains one of the cheapest ways to start a business.

Management: While the presentation and ordering of your products is automated, unless you arrange for your wholesaler to drop ship for you, you will need to set aside an area for inventory and shipping. I hate dealing with shipping, so I have had delivery companies come directly to my house at the end of each day to cut out the last step. Take daily shots of your traffic reports so that you can notice and respond to trends; with this kind of traffic report, you're not concerned about traffic on the freeway, but rather with data about visitors to your site. If need be, test and play with your keywords.

In the beginning, you will be micromanaging your company, doing most tasks yourself; however, if your company grows, you may consider hiring a webmaster and a shipping clerk.

Marketing: Getting your keywords right is essential. Comprehensive descriptions increase your conversion rates (visitors to buyers) tremendously. Using a combination of SEO (search engine optimization) and PPC (Pay per Click) improves traffic. Discount coupons in each package you ship and a good selection of merchandize should lead to increased traffic and repeat sales. See the next section for more on internet marketing; however, if SEO and PPC are Greek to you, you need to either educate yourself or find a partner or employee with internet marketing skills before you start an online business.

8. E-books; From Binders to Bytes.

Somehow I always knew I was going to write. Way back when (no disclosure of exactly when), I tried my hand at it. It was well before the current self-publishing craze, and I thought I might make some good bucks with it. Now don't laugh, but the first book I wrote was about natural aphrodisiacs. I spent a lot of time researching the various natural plants, herbs, and roots that could give your love life some oomph. What a trip. I even got my girlfriend to give the manuscript to a friend who wrote articles for The New York Times.

After this reporter edited the book and returned it to me, I quite frankly didn't know what to do with it. I wish I had it now. Although most people now skip the effort to find a natural stimulant in favor of Viagra or similar pharmaceuticals, my book did contain valuable information, especially for that time. But the question remained: How was I going to get it out to the public? I sent it off to a couple of publishers, and it was summarily rejected. So I tucked it away in a desk drawer and years later went looking for it. No go. It was lost in one of my many moves.

This brings us to the current situation with self-publishing. This is now a business that almost anyone with the ability to tell a story can get into with little money and no overhead. If I had that manuscript today, I could self-publish it in about one hour as an EBook, an option not available when I wrote it. I would put a cover on that sucker and watch some money roll in. (See my book Write with Passion. Sell with Power). Writing EBooks is probably the ultimate for 'icemen' for both creativity and running your own business. On a creative level, it allows for intellectual expression. On an enterprise level, nothing beats creating, owning, and distributing your own product. Ebooks—electronic books—are books that are formatted to be distributed over the internet.

Bulletin Boards, an early method for sending messages en masse electronically that was popular from the early '80s through the mid-'90s, helped pave the way for EBooks as well as the World Wide Web. Commonly used to run software, Bulletin Boards also allowed users to dial in to a server and perform various functions, including downloading material.

However, user-friendly and popular email was perhaps a more important precursor. Although Michael Hart, founder of Project Gutenberg, is often given the credit for inventing EBooks in 1971, earlier efforts to make EBooks a reality include that of teacher Angela Ruíz Robles of Spain, who patented an EBook in 1949, according to Wikipedia.

You probably received this book via instant download.

Books such as this, referred to as self-help or how-to books are always popular sellers.

In the physical world, the number of self-help books in print at any given time is limited, which makes it less likely that a traditional publisher will take on your book.

In the virtual world, the number of self-help titles approaches 100,000. If you include reports, books, manuals, and other formats for digital delivery (CDs), these numbers approach one million. Selling information is big business.

EBooks can be marketed the same way you would market physical products via the internet. However, creating your own product is better than selling items you purchased at wholesale. Once written and copyrighted, the product is yours. It is considered intellectual property, and you can do what you want with it. Further, it is cheaper to deliver than a physical product, and you reap the benefits with residual revenues: you create the book once—the writing and the formatting—and sell it multiple times.

What's required is a fertile mind for creating the content, a website, and a budget for advertising. Advertising is done in various ways. The primary way is using PPC. This PPC, as mentioned earlier, stands for Pay per Click. Google, MSN, and Yahoo all own search engines and allow advertisers to display ads within the search results. So, for example, if an internet user were to search for information about business startups, an advertisement for this book may appear. If a user clicks on my ad, then I pay Google a small fee. No click, no fee.

Other ways to promote your EBook include the use of social sites, writing articles or blogs, joint ventures, and viral marketing. However, the powerhouse in the self-publishing game is Amazon. The system is built to let anyone self-publish and sell. In Write with Passion, I show the steps for virtually formatting and uploading an EBook to the site. It couldn't be easier. The writing is the hard part, but if you take my advice and stick to what you know, you can make it an easier task.

Since publishing my own books, I have learned some useful information. The first piece of advice that I can give you is to eliminate distractions when you sit down to write. This is hard to do. I find myself surfing the internet forever and always procrastinating. For me, this is okay as I write for pleasure without putting pressure on myself. However, if you choose to follow the plan in the Write with Passion and pump out ten books, you need to spend more time writing than surfing.

The second piece of advice I can pass on is that if you decide to publish with Amazon, take advantage of the company's KDP program for promoting your book by making it free for a limited time. You make no money, but the book is counted as a sale, which can help send it straight to the top of the best sellers within your category. This makes it more visible when people are looking for your book.

Lastly, I have chosen to write within one niche, self-help books. Working within a niche helps you focus your energies and apply what you learn on one book to the next one. Just make sure it's a niche with lots of potential: one that has a wide audience and interest level and is expected to grow.

With little money, good use of your time, and patience, you can earn decent bucks writing books.

Funding: The minimal amount of money required to publish EBooks came from savings. If you don't have a computer, you will need one. In addition, you need word processing software and an internet connection.

You can learn more from my book, Write with Passion . . . Sell with Power. Get it at Amazon.

Management: This is an iceman's dream. No fuss, no mess. Occasionally you need to check your statistics on all the sites you use for marketing. Tweak the key words, change the categories, or even consider changing titles. The whole process is self-contained with little management required. In fact, the need for management comes when you are writing. It takes discipline to focus on writing and to control pesky distractions such as phone calls and emails.

Marketing: At the moment, the marketing of your EBooks can be left to one company, Amazon. There are other platforms outlined in my book, Write with Passion . . . Sell with Power; however, the big 'A' does a good job.

Build a website using WordPress to promote and sell your book and make sure you have inbound and outbound links to drive traffic. Consider writing a daily blog on a topic for which you have passion, for posting on your website. You can also post the blog or put a link to it on sites such as Amazon and goodreads.com. Create a writer's profile at Amazon's Author Central. Link all your social or professional sites, including LinkedIn and Facebook, to Amazon. Link your E-commerce sites to the same writer's profile. Use some of the content in your books on all your sites. Finally, if you get invited to do a book signing because you also offer a paper-and-ink version of your book through a print on demand program . . . don't turn it down!

9. The Business of Hobbies.

If you don't have one . . . get one. With all the free time you will generate as an iceman, you will need one. The money that you may make with your hobby is just a bonus. I see it as a way to generate freshness and creativity. It's a way to take on life while living 'the life.' The hobby can be anything from collecting vintage watches or stamps, photography, traveling, or hang gliding. It doesn't matter. Along the way, if it somehow generates money . . . great!

It did for me. I started collecting vintage watches, and it turned into a moneymaker. In the beginning, I had no desire to make money. I bought the watches to wear and enjoyed the numerous comments I would get.

Something about wearing a vintage gold watch

attracted the ladies. It never failed. I'd be across the room at a party and out of nowhere a woman would come up and ask the time. It was an excuse to see the watch, and I used it as an excuse to see them. Collecting and wearing anything with aesthetic value arouses the senses of people who appreciate beauty.

This hobby started many years ago when I was given a gold-filled watch as a birthday present. The watch itself wasn't anything exceptional, but something clicked. I got curious about the makings and guts of the things and went crazy reading all about them. Discovering the intricacies, the history, and the values had me hooked.

At one point, I was buying a watch every month. Some were new, but most were vintage watches. I discovered that if I bought right, I could sell for a profit. I had both men and woman asking where I got them from and in many encounters offered me cash on the spot. If I felt ready to part with the watch and was short of cash, I would sell. I collected watches and sold them in this low-key manner for several years before I discovered the internet and the vast number of people who were into the same hobby.

That changed things. My hobby now became a real business. The startup costs were minimal. I quickly secured a domain name related to vintage watches, set up a few web pages with a comments section, and it was off to the races. The commentary section in the pages is particularly important. People want to know that you are trustworthy and know what you are talking about. Getting good photos of the watches can be a challenge. However, photography is one of my hobbies, so I quickly learned how to shoot watches as a product. I selected some of the first watches I acquired, got the descriptions from the various watch books in my library, and posted the photos and descriptions online.

What a trip! Watches I bought years earlier were in high demand. Even the ones of little value eventually sold. I never lost a dime on a watch. In fact, it was an easy way to contribute a sizeable amount of cash to my 'Shove It Fund'.

When you decide on a hobby, consider it something to do for pleasure. As you learn more about it, you may want to consider it as a vehicle to generate cash. The biggest problem with collecting is the supply. Make sure you manage your resources to keep up a steady supply. In my case, I made friends with watch repairers and pawn shop owners, and I even had a guy visit my office once a month to show me his 'new vintage watches.'

With other hobbies such as surfing, hang gliding, and hiking, it is easy to turn your passion into a business.

You are now the expert and your knowledge can be used to promote supplies, clothing, and any other items used in your hobby. As a bonus, try writing a guide about your hobby and join the millions who have been self-published.

Funding: This was ongoing. Each month I would use my savings or extra cash to purchase a watch. I decided early on to stick within a certain price range. Taking some of the profits to buy additional pieces is the natural thing to do.

Management: This requires you to manage only yourself as you build websites with excellent descriptions and photos. Check your web stats and keywords to make sure they are performing properly. Shipping is easy for these lightweight items, but it must include tracking and be fast.

Marketing: Getting the word out about your hobby requires a lot of word of mouth. Having a business card saying you are a watch dealer helps. When using the websites to promote, make sure to mention that you are a dealer and that you both buy and sell watches. This gives you the opportunity to build your inventory.

10. Teaching English as a Business

According to the European Union's website, English is the most studied language among the 27 countries in the union: 95 percent of upper secondary and general studies schools and 82 percent of primary and secondary schools in the EU provide English classes.

In Norway, every primary and secondary school offers English, with Italy and Spain close behind at 99 percent. The lowest country percentage is France, at 43 percent.

For the upper secondary and general schools, Belgium, Bulgaria, and France lead the pack at 100%, with

Norway coming in at the lower end at 45%. This lower number for Norway probably means that children there master English in the lower grade levels, where it is taught in all schools, so English classes are less needed for older students.

I recently discovered that France's effort at the secondary level seems to be paying off big time. On a recent trip to Paris, I was astonished at the number of people speaking fluent English.

This leads me to tell you about the enormous need for English teachers in European countries. Hence, this is an excellent opportunity for any iceman. The numbers above give you an idea as to what is going on, especially in the upper secondary and general category. This group is comprised of mostly adults, most being advanced students and business professionals. In the chapter on Foreign Horizons, I tried to give you information about which countries are the easiest to do business in. A lot of those countries are in Europe.

If you choose the business of teaching English in one of the more populated European countries, you are virtually assured success. The European Union in some cases will even fund you.

Currently, this is one of my main businesses. A local resident approached me, asking me to partner with him on a company that would supply English teachers to professionals. He was a former student of mine, and I think he liked what I was doing. The truth is I barely remembered him from the class. His participation had been fairly minimal until we had a discussion on phrasal verbs. When we got to the phrasal verb 'hang up,' he became animated. He wanted to know the different meanings of 'hang up' because it was his secretary's favorite expression. Well, she wasn't using it as a phrasal verb referring to disconnected phone calls; she was instead saying he had a lot of issues! Those funky phrasal verbs are a nuisance in our language. They should be banned.

Anyway, when he approached me, I did remember the secretary bit and now started to think this guy was an iceman. Sure enough, he was. He owned a couple of garages and a beauty salon.

The entire negotiating period took two weeks. I was brought in as an associate sharing the profits at 50 percent. In addition, I had the right of first refusal if someone came along and offered to buy the company.

Further I negotiated the right to keep 75 percent of my personal billing. (See below). The paperwork took an additional two weeks. While all this was going on, my partner-to-be had submitted a loan proposal to the Union that was approved within a month. We now had the funding. All we needed was the model for doing the work.

This was quite straightforward as the targets were professionals, and we wanted to send teachers directly to their business as opposed to incurring the overhead to set up a school. It is the same model as with IT consulting, so it was right up my alley.

As in the software consulting business, you again essentially become a payroll company, once teachers are placed. The idea is to put people on billing and receive a premium for doing so. You or a salesperson goes out to a client, qualifies the need, and finds a teacher fitting the needs of the client. The numbers don't match those in IT consulting, but the same model works. For example, you charge the client 40 euros per hour and pay the teacher 20 euros per hour. You now have a gross profit of 20 euros. There may be cases where you can charge more, but for illustration purposes let's stick with 20 euros as the average.

If you net 20 euros per hour on every teacher you put to work, you will make a decent living. Further, this is passive income. Let's take the scenario of having 20 teachers working for you. If each teacher works 4 hours a day, 20 hours per week, and we assume we have 20 work days each month (love that number 20), your gross profit is 32,000 euros per month.

Actually, that is more than a decent living. However, remember you have some expenses. You may have an office, computer systems, software, secretary, and commissions to be paid to salespeople. So what? All these things are pretty much fixed, but true net is still terrific. As I said, the business is essentially a payroll company. If you manage to get the funding upfront as we did, you are on your way. What remains are organizational and billing systems to be put in place.

Be ready to send bills out to clients at month's end. Collect the time sheets from the teachers and collect the money from the clients. You have to love it! This is an iceman's dream!

Funding: The funding was in place from loans secured from the European Union. Some of my personal funds were used to create a business website.

Management: Make your salesperson responsible not only for selling but also for managing each account. Our salesperson occasionally visits each account for feedback and to explore the opportunity for additional business. The back office is micromanaged with the emphasis on recruiting and billing. The systems are all integrated, allowing for spot checks on requirements, cash flow, and projections.

Marketing: A website is a must, and interestingly, at the moment, there is remarkably little in the way of competition. Concentrating on teaching professionals and executives helps focus the goal of the business. Handing out business cards and placing an occasional classified ad in local business magazines will bring new leads and contacts. The company's visibility is improved by having a salesman.

11. Back to the Bar!

Okay, go grab a cocktail and read this while you relax with your Kindle. The dream came true. The bar was not at seaside but in a densely populated European city. We opened the bar in three short months. The opening was New Year's Eve, with one hell of a party. I actually had been in New York two weeks earlier when I was notified about the opening date. Of course, I was in contact with my new partner on a daily basis.

During the build-out and approval period, I was back and forth to Europe three or four times. My presence wasn't needed to facilitate the process. On the occasions when I was there, I had the opportunity to visit principal cities throughout Europe. When I was needed, it was to consult with the landlord and suppliers and to organize some matters that my partner couldn't handle. Still these things were minor, and I had a fair amount of time on my hands. What a blast! I was free to travel, all under the guise of potentially owning a business in Europe. This was the ultimate escape for me.

Opening a bar is difficult, and glamour should be an afterthought. We got lucky because we were able to buy the license from an existing business. The rules say the company must be put in a local resident's name. This was solved when the wife of my partner agreed to be the signer. After doing further research and talking to good contacts, we decided to organize the business in a way that allowed us to pay a flat fee (tax) each month, rather than a percentage of sales. This saved us tons of money. It is essential if you try to set up a business anywhere outside of your native country to look into the tax rules and the different ways to organize a business.

The transaction was treated as a simple transfer of assets. So in addition to the license, we inherited everything in the place, from cocktail glasses and beer mugs to chairs and bar stools. The most notable piece in the bar was a 10-foot marble bar and an impressive wall mirror behind it. The only real work we had to do was to paint and clear out some junk in the front window. After deciding on a theme, we bought and framed photos representing New York. Overall it was a good, painless transaction; we wound up with a great bar with a fantastic theme. Together with the new theme we developed a new and exotic (for the area) cocktail menu.

Speaking of area, the bar's location was one of the keys to its success. Based on extensive research, we chose the fringes of an area frequented by many tourists. This goes back to the axiom for real estate: Location, location, location. Equally important to the bar's success was my selection of a partner. He was a trustworthy friend who was also a famous musician, which virtually guaranteed success upon opening.

Funding: The money for doing this deal came from savings and residual income from my main business in New York.

Management: Micro. Running a cash-based business requires an owner or trusted manager to be present at all times. Don't think this business is one for absentee ownership. I was lucky in that I had a trusted partner. Keeping an accurate inventory of liquor is important.

Hiring almost comes down to instinct, but all references should be checked. Even after checking references, you still can't be sure about your employees until they begin to work for you. I hired a bartender who was sniffing everything he could get his hands on, including coffee grinds reserved for those trying to sober up before they left the bar. Another bar owner trusted one of his main workers with the key and later found out that the guy was opening the bar on Sundays and keeping all the profits. Stay close.

Marketing: This was relatively easy as we had a good location and plenty of 'walk-ins.' In addition, since my partner was famous, word got around and pretty soon the bar was packed every night with people interested in seeing and talking to him. We also created a different atmosphere by playing American blues, jazz, and rock and roll. The menu, as mentioned, was designed to provide the locals with drinks that were unavailable at other bars. All of these things created a positive buzz, and we had extensive coverage with the local and national press. When things slowed down, we printed flyers offering two for one drinks with different theme nights.

12. Conclusion: L.U.S.T. for Living!

"Balance is the key: I need to be successful in my career to feel fulfilled, be surrounded by people I care about to share it with, and have my health to be able to do the things I love to do!"
- Kiana Tom

I hope this book gives you some ideas for startups while helping you avoid some pitfalls.

My journey is unique, and yours will be too. Once you begin the practice of looking for opportunities and developing an eye for business, your life will change. You will need your iceman fix for intellectual reasons or for survival. You can easily draw the parallel to actors or artists. As they mature, they continually seek new challenges with the desire to stretch themselves creatively and to sustain their fan base while reaching new fans.

As you get older, you will no longer want the option of working for someone else. If you wanted to reenter the job market, you would need to reinvent yourself. As an iceman, you won't need to do this. You just need to continue your journey by keeping abreast of the changes in business and technology.

In the beginning of my journey, technology played a minor role in pushing my companies in the direction of real profits. I relied heavily on human and creative resources to manage and promote the companies. If you follow the progression of the companies I started, you will notice less and less reliance on human capital. Today technology has allowed icemen to go it alone.

Technology is a solid asset in a range of endeavors, from launching an E-commerce store to writing and publishing books. Even with the English Business School, technology has eliminated the need to hire extra staff for the back office operations. Database systems, billing systems, and other software have made the job of a business owner a whole lot easier. When you throw in the potential of the internet as a marketing tool, the possibilities for success are even greater.

Embrace technology and incorporate the following basic formula for your iceman journey. I call it the L.U.S.T. for living.

The 'L' in the formula calls for you to learn a trade or any discipline that will allow you to proceed as an iceman with the confidence that you could always get a job.

The 'U' in the formula calls for you to 'use' what you have learned and apply it to your new business.

The 'S' in this prescription calls for you to share your knowledge with co-workers and future employees. Share what you know about systems and organization.

Having employees share their own experiences builds trust. Sharing your iceman experiences as the boss is paramount to success. Ultimately this makes your venture into the world of startups more prosperous.

The last letter, 'T,' means to teach whenever you can. On a personal level, this can be not only immensely satisfying but also potentially lucrative if you choose to write an EBook. At the business level, writing a training manual or teaching your staff the nuances of the business limits mistakes. It also defines responsibilities, while allowing decisions to be made by the appropriate people. Ultimately, this leads the iceman to more freedom and independence.

One of the best endorsements as an iceman I ever received was from my own wife. It was my birthday. As I passed through the front door at home, my wife kissed me and told me to go to my desk. There I found an envelope containing a round-trip ticket and a voucher for a four-star hotel in Paris.

Upon further inspection, I found a note saying "Happy Birthday, You are free as you want to be…have fun…you deserve it. Love, me and the kids."

Bon Voyage!

13. Bonus Chapter: Corporate Speak

"Think like a wise man but communicate in the language of the people."
- William Butler Yeats

If you've sent or received memos or reports sprinkled with words and phrases such as corporate vision and deliverables and key metrics and service culture, then you may be fluent already in Corporate Speak. If you haven't, I'll walk you through a few of them, just in case your Iceman path includes negotiating with representatives of any (BIM.Corp), Big Important Mega Corporation.

By Corporate Speak, I'm not talking about the jargon that is distinct for each type of business, whether law or mechanics or banking or bartending, but rather the language that can sometimes seem like a creeping mold in big corporations.

Let me give you an example of why I dislike Corporate Speak, which can sometimes come across as Elitist Speak:

While working in personnel placement, I represented a well-qualified job candidate who would be an asset at any company. I sent his résumé to a large, long-established bank based in Europe. I eventually received a letter from someone in the personnel department of this well-known financial institution. It was overflowing with Corporate Speak stressing the bank's guiding principles and its action by committee; the paragraph saying the bank was interested in interviewing my candidate was buried way at the bottom.

By the time the letter arrived, my firm and I had pocketed a nice fee for placing my candidate in happy employment with a mid-sized firm. Why hadn't the bank's representative picked up the phone and set up an interview with this gem of a candidate before the opportunity was lost, instead of sending a letter dripping with pretentiousness? When you're too big to get things done, perhaps you're just too big.

Fortunately, those creating startups will generally enjoy relationships with smaller, more agile trading partners. As a result, you'll be able to communicate in real time with these partners.

The following are some common Corporate Speak terms and phrases and their definitions. Realize that Corporate Speak can be used as a negotiating tactic; don't be intimidated. These definitions should help if you have to spend time communicating with lovers of corporate verbosity.

Here are some of the terms I remember from the bank's letter:

Corporate Vision: This is simply a laundry list of things the company is trying to accomplish.

Foundation of Culture or Corporate Culture: What does the corporation value? If you're cynical, you might see this as a corporation's propaganda to get employees to think and believe in a way that supports the company's success. Usually the Foundation of Culture is described in the mission statement, but there may also be an unwritten Corporate Culture; for instance, to sit in the big chair, you may first have to put in ridiculous hours as a low-level executive.

Out of the Box or Outside the Box: If someone suggests that you think outside the box, that person wants you to get more creative.

Reputational Consequences: You likely understand the meaning of 'reputation' and of 'consequences.' To look at 'reputational consequences' simply means to ask: How will this affect the corporation's reputation?
In the Loop: You know what's going on; you're informed of decisions or involved in making them. When executives fail with a project, they sometimes say they were "out of the loop."

Core Client Service Values: A set of values derived from the corporate vision and culture.

Key Metrics: A way for a company to measure success according to its own internal measuring system or model.

Hard Copy: Paper output, as opposed to digital output, which is called "soft copy."

Action Item: An item on which action will be taken—yep, it's that simple. Some possibilities are discussed forever without a decision to act, so they don't become Action Items.

Touch Base: One of my favorites, it simply means contact me.

Here are a few more juicy, corny, and over the top examples of Corporate Speak.

Deliverables: These should be included with the product when it is, uh, delivered. In the tangible sense, this might be a battery that should be delivered with a remote sensor. Within the walls of the corporation, these may be reports or summaries highlighting the milestones (finished segments) for a project.

Disconnect: In Corporate Speak, this can be seen as a non sequitur. If, for example, the boss inquires about the latest sales results and I reply, "You know, I caught a giant catfish this weekend," this is a 'disconnect.' My response isn't even close to the subject. Sometimes it indicates a difference in what one department is doing as opposed to another.

Diversity Awareness/Training: If an employee's words or actions indicate he/she doesn't value different categories of people equally—whether because of race, gender, or other factors—that employee may be required to attend diversity awareness or training. If you have a startup, you may not have a formal program for diversity awareness, but that doesn't mean you can be oblivious to an employee's prejudice, since that worker's words or deeds can impact the reputation of your business.

Fast Track: An individual who shows talent, gumption, and ambition may be boosted up the ladder of success faster than others can climb the rungs. A project can also be 'Fast Tracked' with actions expedited so the work can be completed quickly.

Hit a Home Run: One of many sports metaphors indicating the launch of a successful product or service.

Key Enabler: An employee who receives the most credit for a project.

Major Account: In my journey, all accounts were major; however, in the corporate world, these are 20 percent of your accounts that bring in 80 percent of the business. If these clients sneeze, you come running with a Kleenex and a free prescription for any drug that can reduce discomfort.

Off-Line: To most of us this means doing things without being connected to the internet. In the halls of executives it means speaking off the record away from the current setting. In other words…a meeting.

Outsourcing/Offshoring: Companies reduce labor and production costs by using independent contractors who receive no employee benefits, by hiring overseas workers or companies to handle specific projects, such as writing computer code, and by sending manufacturing overseas.

Overhead: No need to look. Overhead is the cost of running the corporation—everything from office space to staples.

Own: In corporate halls, executives who take responsibility for their work 'own' the results and can never claim they were 'out of the loop.'

Pre-Meeting: A meeting before a meeting or even before that meeting. 'In the loop' participants decide on what to say at the actual meeting so they don't embarrass themselves and can accomplish a desired result.

Talk Track: A script committed to memory by the sales team in order to create a single focus for products or services. This helps prevent babbling.

Up Selling: Selling additional products that may not be needed but are seemingly related to the first product.
Value Added: Bonus benefits or features added to existing products to make customers feel they are getting something extra with their purchase.

14. References

Greedy Bastards by Dylan Ratigan

23 Things They Don't Tell You About Capitalism by Ha-Joon Chang

How to Write a Business Plan for Astonishing Results. In Just 3 Days! By Vinil Ramdev

The Art of Funding a Startup by Paul Graham

Success Secrets of the Online Marketing Superstars by Mitch Meyerson

How to Write Web Pages on Any Topic Fast by Adam Kosloff

Top Ranked: Promoting Your Small Business on the Internet by John Huegel

The Ultimate Guide to Google AdWords by Perry Marshall

Success Quotes: 129 Gems from the World's Most Famous People by Christine J. Collins

Damn! Why Didn't I Write That? How Ordinary People are Raking in $100,000.00 or More Writing Nonfiction Books & How You Can Too! By Marc

McCutcheon

The Elements of Style by William Strunk and E. B. White

265 Troubleshooting Strategies for Writing Nonfiction by Barbara Fine Clouse

15. About The Author

"Listen to your heart . . . Follow that dream!"
Me

Writer, teacher, entrepreneur, traveler, and motivational speaker: E.J. Kelly, also known as 'the happy hombre,' has worn all of these hats. A native of New York, he discovered his entrepreneurial spirit while young, starting and running several successful businesses in the United States before moving to Europe.

One of his U.S. startups provided headhunting/human resources services to IT professionals. He also owned and operated a real estate company, a travel agency, and a bagel delicatessen considered one of the best in the New York area.

After becoming an expatriate, Kelly continued his success by opening the Manhattan Martini Bar in Madrid. In 2002, the well-respected "Lo Mejor De La Gastronomía" (the best of gastronomy) named the Manhattan Martini Bar the best cocktail bar in Spain. This guide by Rafael García Santos also ranks great restaurants, dishes, delicacies, and wines.

E.J. Kelly now focuses most of his time on living life fully, writing and publishing self-help and how-to books, and teaching "Native English" and Business English. He occasionally accepts invitations to give motivational speeches to students and business professionals.

His interests include cinema, reading, photography, vintage watch collecting, business, teaching methods, foreign cultures, travel, and languages—but not necessarily in that order.

Follow that dream!

Other Books By The Author

* Write with Passion...Sell with Power. A how-to guide on writing, self-publishing, and marketing self-help guides.

* Treasures in Time: How to Profit Collecting Vintage Watches. A down-to-earth guide on how to buy and sell vintage watches for profit.

* Treasures in Time 2: Profit from Vintage Quartz and Electric Watches: A follow-up to Treasures in Time, for more fun and profit.

* Teaching English Abroad: A How to Guide. Thinking about a career teaching English overseas? This guide will show you how.

* Teach English Abroad to Spanish Students. With more than 500 million Spanish speakers ready to learn English, this guide shows you how to teach them.

* Fun-E-book Dictionary: Learn Ebook and Internet Terms. For those who want to make money online, enjoy a fun walk through self-publishing and internet terminology.

If you have enjoyed this book and found it useful, please take time to write a review, no matter how short or long. For reviewers who are also writers, I would be happy to review your book in return. Just drop me a line!

Thanks.

Thehappyhombrepress@gmail.com
Thehappyhombre@gmail.com

Disclaimer and Legal Notices

The information contained in this guide represents the view of the author as of the date of publication. The market is dynamic and has rapidly changing conditions. The author maintains the right to alter his opinions. The guide is for informational purposes only.

Every attempt has been made to verify the information provided. The author assumes no responsibility for errors, inaccuracies, or omissions. If legal advice is needed, the services of a fully qualified professional should be sought.

The methods and results used for selling may not apply to the average person. A person's success is based on individual background, dedication, desire, and motivation. As with any business, including the creation and selling of products or services, there is no guarantee you will earn money. However, I believe that you will succeed if you make every effort.

Happy Trails . . .

www.ingramcontent.com/pod-product-compliance
Lightning Source LLC
Chambersburg PA
CBHW051917170526
45168CB00001B/429